HISTORY THROUGH THE HEADSETS

INSIDE NOTRE DAME'S PLAYOFF RUN DURING THE CRAZIEST SEASON IN COLLEGE FOOTBALL HISTORY

JOHN MAHONEY

AND

REED GREGORY

TRIUMPH
BOOKS

Library of Congress Cataloging-in-Publication Data available upon request

This book is available in quantity at special discounts for your group or organization. For further information, contact:

Triumph Books LLC
814 North Franklin Street
Chicago, Illinois 60610
Phone: (312) 337-0747
www.triumphbooks.com

Printed in U.S.A.
ISBN: 978-1-62937-968-5
Interior design and editorial production by Alex Lubertozzi
Photos courtesy of Jeffrey Myers, Rachel Pincus, and Matt Taylor

CONTENTS

FOREWORD

....

by BRIAN KELLY

In my 30-plus years of being a head coach, there has never been a season like we experienced in 2020. With all that COVID-19 brought with it, it was at times inconceivable that we would be able to play a football season, but with the unwavering support from our University of Notre Dame leadership, we were able to move forward and play a season that was unforgettable for more than just the unusual circumstances under which it was played.

We will look back and remember this 2020 Notre Dame Football season as one that had an unrelenting brotherhood. Both players and staff alike made so many sacrifices for the greater good, and it paid huge dividends. From our unanimous All-American in Jeremiah Owusu-Koramoah to the group of walk-ons who make up WOPU Nation, the commitment was the same in our efforts to not only have a season, but to have a highly successful one at that.

For the second time in three seasons, our program earned an invitation to the College Football Playoff, becoming one of just five programs to make multiple appearances on our game's biggest stage. We got there in large part due to our thrilling double-overtime win over Clemson in the 2020 college football season's most-watched regular season game. A big road win over nationally ranked North Carolina and a home victory over Florida State were other highlights on our way to appearing in our first, and likely last, ACC Championship Game.

That type of success does not come without many unheralded contributions, most notably from our walk-ons. Their willingness to give of themselves without the guarantee of playing time or recognition requires an uncommon fortitude. But our walk-ons are special, and the culture of WOPU Nation has created bonds in our program that are absolutely vital to our overall success.

Reed Gregory and John Mahoney perfectly embody what it takes to be a member of WOPU Nation. They are hardworking, highly intelligent, humble men who are willing to go to great lengths to better the team, regardless of the task. Their relentless work ethic in practice and in the weight room made us better. That is where they earned the respect of teammates and coaches. Because of the amount of trust we placed in Reed and John, they were able to really carve their niche in our program as signal callers.

Now, you might not know or understand the importance of the role of the signal callers, but it requires players who are level-headed, reliable, and have the ability to think on their feet. Not only does a signaler have to recall each play's signals within seconds, they also have to ensure every player who could potentially touch the field knows what each signal means. As the only means of communication between the coaches and the players on the field, it requires the coaches to have complete trust in the guys on the headsets—and Reed and John were a great fit in this role.

Reed and John were always prepared for both practice and games, and because of the work they put into doing the job at the highest level, we were able to achieve the standard of communication it takes to be an elite football team.

On top of that, they are far better players than most would give them credit for being, and I know neither one ever shied away from a challenge. It is extremely difficult for a walk-on to earn time on the field at Notre Dame, and these two both did that. But even if they hadn't, their imprint was more than stamped on this program.

As great as Reed and John were at being our trusted signal callers, they also brought some personality to our locker room. I have enjoyed having conversations with them about topics unrelated to football, including their passions outside of the sport, family updates, and happenings in their hometowns. Additionally, they valued the importance of working hard in the classroom, as evidenced by their inclusion on the 2020–21 ACC Academic Honor Roll.

This 2020 edition of Notre Dame Football was a very special group to me because of the strong character they possessed, and Reed and John are the epitome of that as much as anyone in our program. I am glad that two of the people who were behind the scenes for many of the biggest moments of our 2020 campaign found the opportunity to tell the story of a season that won't be forgotten anytime soon.

Reed and John are true Notre Dame men, and I am eager to see all of the amazing things they accomplish moving forward.

—Brian Kelly
Dick Corbett Head Football Coach
at the University of Notre Dame
July 2021

PROLOGUE

THE FINAL MOMENTS

And, just like that, it was over. As Ian Book's pass—intended for senior receiver Avery Davis—skittered to the turf at AT&T Stadium, a reality that had been apparent to almost everybody for the last couple of hours became final and irrefutable. Notre Dame's 2020 season, which seemed simultaneously chaotic and pure, improbable and inevitable, exhilarating and gut-wrenching, had drawn to a close. After the perfunctory handshakes and congratulations—which had looked different all year given the circumstances surrounding public health—the 2020 Fighting Irish left the field for the final time. This was the last time that Notre Dame legends like Book (the winningest quarterback in program history), Robert Hainsey, Liam Eichenberg, Butkus Award winner Jeremiah Owusu-Koramoah, and so many others would ever don the blue and gold. This was a group that had led the Irish from the ashes of a 4–8 season in 2016 to 43 wins and, for the first time in program history, four consecutive 10-win seasons between 2017 and 2020—all while graduating from Notre Dame and accumulating tremendous personal accolades along the way. Despite the loss, there was no denying that they had made their mark in the already illustrious annals of Fighting Irish history.

With that being said, however, there was little doubt that each of these players would continue their careers at the next level. In fact, the Irish had nine players selected in the NFL Draft that spring—their largest total since 1994. Eichenberg, Owusu-Koramoah, and Aaron Banks were all selected in the second round—by Miami, Cleveland, and San Francisco respectively—while Hainsey joined the defending Super Bowl champion Tampa Bay Buccaneers in the third round. Additionally, Tommy Tremble heard his name called in the third round and became a Carolina Panther, and Book found himself heading to New Orleans as the Saints' fourth-round pick. For another group of players, however, this was the last time they would *ever* strap on the pads. And though the majority of them didn't see the field against Alabama or Clemson, the overwhelming sense of finality that came with walking off the field for the last time, finding themselves suddenly ex-football players, was something that was impossible to prepare for. For them, it wasn't the end of a season; it was the end of a career that had likely begun many years before—one that included a myriad of setbacks, lucky breaks, and experiences they never could have imagined when they stepped on campus as freshmen.

JOHN: As much as I told myself I was ready for it, I couldn't help but tear up as I left the field. I'd started playing football when I was eight years old, and there I was—a few days short of turning 22—and it was done. If it had been a normal bowl game, it might have been easier, but I truly thought going in that this wasn't going to be it for us. I'd be lying if I said it wasn't really tough to have it end the way it did.

REED: I cried the first time I thought my football career was over, and that was my senior year of high school. After reminiscing about the trials and tribulations that had to take place for me to get to this point, there was no way I would be able to hold back the tears. Acknowledging it was the end was the most challenging part. The end to thousands of hours of strenuous effort and work devoted to a single goal: winning a championship. A goal that we had just fallen short of.

Somewhere beneath the heartbreak, however, there were things that the Irish faithful could certainly be proud of. It had been a valiant effort. Behind by two scores at halftime, the Irish had done what few other teams could throughout the season by simply staying in the game—holding the vaunted Crimson Tide offense to just 10 points in the second half. Following a touchdown that stemmed from an Ian Book interception, however, Alabama took a commanding 28–7 lead that the Irish were ultimately unable to surmount. An Irish touchdown with a minute to play was little solace. The ensuing onside kick recovery inspired what was left of the crowd, but had little practical impact. Never mind that the Fighting Irish had held Alabama to its lowest point total in two years—an achievement that persisted through the following Monday's National Championship Game—or that they had defied prevailing wisdom by covering the 19-point spread set by the oddsmakers in Vegas. It was over—the Tide moved on to the title game in Miami, while the Irish, after a somber, tearful series of good-byes in the locker room, headed to the Fort Worth airport for a lonely, quiet flight back to South Bend. Upon their arrival, they were greeted—predictably, given their destination—by below-freezing temperatures and a fresh covering of snow.

Sports are often cruel in that seasons are almost always defined by the way they finish. The bowl system has historically kept college football somewhat immune to that, but—thanks in no small part to the advent of the College Football Playoff seven seasons prior—it was tough to discern a silver lining as Brian Kelly's team left that locker room in Arlington. Over cold barbecue in a modified parking lot somewhere beneath AT&T Stadium, players and coaches alike struggled to find much to say. Never mind that they had managed to achieve the 23rd undefeated regular season in school history, that they had beaten the No. 1 team in the country on their home turf for the first time in 27 years, or even that they'd managed to play a full season as a pandemic ravaged the globe and upended virtually every aspect of everyday life. At Notre Dame, in 2020 as it always has been, there is one goal—a national championship. To have worked so hard, sacrificed so much, and come so close only to fall short was heartbreaking for all those involved.

> **JOHN:** Following bowl games, whether we win or lose, there usually is a gathering back at the hotel for players, coaches, and their families. It's always a good time and provides the opportunity for some closure on what was usually a memorable season. Obviously, COVID prevented such an event from happening—making the trip home that much more painful. I've been on some quiet plane rides, but nothing like this. It was almost impossible to think of anything to say, so most of us simply didn't.

With that being said, however, the memories made by all involved are certain to last long beyond their time on campus. It was a season that saw traditional rivalry matchups with Navy and USC, both universally considered to be among the longest-standing and best rivalries in the country, wiped from the schedule. Trips to Ireland and Lambeau Field were canceled, and attendance at Notre Dame Stadium was limited to students, faculty, and the families of players and coaches—who, at around 10,000 strong, created a decided home-field advantage but were nevertheless a far cry from the 77,622 that fill the stands on a normal fall Saturday in South Bend. Despite this, the season included a victory over No. 1–ranked

Clemson, a second appearance in the College Football Playoff, and an undefeated romp through a conference schedule for the first time in program history. The Irish were able to achieve all this through not one but two complete shutdowns of the program, repressive COVID testing and rules that seemed to dictate every element of players' daily lives, as well as social and political turmoil that engulfed the United States. It was perhaps the most unusual college football season in recent memory—an incredible ride that involved a tremendous amount of twists and turns. And though the most memorable parts occurred in the months of November, December, and January, the story began months before—in a world much simpler than the one it finished in.

THE OUTBREAK—QUARANTINI

A s the calendar turned to March and the weather in Northern Indiana began to suggest that spring was, in fact, on its way, the 2020 Fighting Irish took the field for the first time, opening spring practice in the still-new Irish Athletic Center on March 5. NCAA rules grant universities just 15 practices in the spring, but they represent a significant opportunity for evaluation, player development, and team-building. As anyone who has been around college football can tell you, any great season gets its start months before, during spring ball. Given this—and eager to improve on the previous season's 11–2 finish—the Irish took the field with vigor and excitement, eager to begin defining the characteristics of Notre Dame's 133rd football team. The season-opening trip to Ireland seemed impossibly distant at the time, but the anticipation was palpable. After all, the team returned its quarterback, entire offensive line, and a number of playmakers on defense. Expectations were high, both inside and outside the program.

Up to that point, head strength coach Matt Balis had led them through an arduous eight weeks of winter training, complete with the "St. Valentine's Day Massacre" and "Dominant Mindset Day"—workouts that incorporated a specific theme, like accountability, love, or trust, and almost always included strategically placed trash cans for players unable to retain the contents of their stomachs in the face of such intense exercise. Winter workouts—an afterthought among most fans and casual observers of the program—are an integral component of Notre Dame's preparation and include perhaps some of the most physically demanding challenges the players will face all year.

> **JOHN:** Ask any of us—those winter workouts are the bane of our existence through January and February. It's always freezing cold, you often have to be there long before the sun comes up, and Coach Balis puts us through the most difficult workouts I've ever been a part of. As a Notre Dame football player, you can't earn your stripes in the fall until you've suffered through a South Bend winter with the strength staff.

> **REED:** The first two to three weeks of the training program are the toughest. Waking up before 6:00 AM every morning, trudging to the gym through the blistering wind and deep snow. I remember sitting in my chair in front of my locker, looking around at everyone, seeing their glazed-over eyes and bed head. I used to chuckle, thinking how ridiculous this whole process was. But as the calendar flipped, everyone started to get into a rhythm. The morning moods changed from feelings of desperation and gloom to energy and alacrity.

As is often the case with the first practice after a long layoff, Practice No. 1 was devoted to shaking off the rust and getting players acclimated to football movements again. Per NCAA rules, the team was only allowed to wear helmets—no other pads—thus eliminating any significant physical contact from the day's practice plan. Instead, the coaches focused heavily on individual drill work prior to entering into some controlled competitive situations. It moved fast, some younger players had the chance to display the improvements they had made, and—most importantly—there were no major injuries. It was still too early to tell, but it was hard not to think that the 2020 Irish were off to a solid start.

The following day, the team got together for weightlifting and meetings before being released on Spring Break, which is always an exciting time for a group of guys exhausted from weeks of strenuous exercise and tired of the "permacloud" that seems to rest over St. Joseph County in the months of January and February. After classes finished, players began to scatter across the country for a well-deserved and much-anticipated week off—some headed home, some headed to Nashville, while others traveled to Las Vegas, Miami, and other places across the country. At that point, COVID-19 was an afterthought. Save for some stories of isolated cases in Washington and New York, it seemed to be a problem that existed primarily outside the United States. Students studying abroad in Europe had been sent home the week before, but there was still a prevailing sense that it was something for the rest of the world to deal with. After all, Americans had lived through outbreaks of the Bird Flu, Swine Flu, Zika Virus, and Ebola, and the overwhelming majority of them hadn't noticed much change in their day-to-day lives. Suffice it to say, then, that the coronavirus was far from the minds of most of the students leaving South Bend on Friday, March 6.

JOHN: It's a little embarrassing to even say this now, but as we left town that day, none of us took COVID that seriously—and certainly never could have imagined that it would develop into the crisis that it did. Reed and I were driving to Nashville, where I met up with a former teammate, Grant Hammann. He works in medical sales, and mentioned to me that the hospital where he spends a lot of his time had preemptively established a COVID response unit—despite the fact that Nashville wasn't dealing with an overwhelming number of cases at that point. I'd certainly never heard of anything like that before, and though I was still unaware of how intense it would become, I started to have a sneaking suspicion that this might become a bigger deal than I had anticipated.

After spending the weekend in Nashville, a substantial contingent of Notre Dame students headed down Interstate 65 toward Panama City Beach—a popular spring break destination for students across the Midwest and South. From their perspective, everything had gone according to plan, but they arrived in Florida living in a different world than the one they had left in Indiana on Friday. Colleges and universities across America had started to shut down, advising their students to return home rather than come back to campus after spring break. Sporting events, including mainstays like conference basketball tournaments, had announced that they would play in front of empty arenas before canceling altogether. In just a few days, American society had been turned on its head, leaving many people frightened and unaware of what the immediate future held. For college students simply hoping to enjoy their time off, it added an element of uncertainty few of them could have anticipated just a week prior.

REED: Although I didn't know it at the time, I had caught the coronavirus that March in Panama City Beach, Florida. At the time, there were no mask mandates anywhere, and all areas open to the general public were at max capacity. A friend on the trip with me had gotten sick earlier in the week. The rest of us jokingly implied that he had gotten COVID-19. We thought it was funny. Two weeks after the trip, my parents had me get tested for COVID and antibodies. I tested negative for COVID and positive for antibodies. After the second round of antibody testing, my family and I were sure that I had contracted the disease in Florida. I was fortunate to be asymptomatic and especially thankful that I did not pass it on to my family while I was home.

After a few days of anticipation, the news came that Notre Dame—like most other schools across the country, had decided to send their students home rather than welcome them back following spring break. Until at least April 13, campus would be closed and classes were to be held entirely online. And though the football program initially hoped to keep the team around during the quarantine, those plans were quickly dashed as well. The annual Blue & Gold game was canceled, and as of Wednesday, March 11, Notre Dame Football was on pause until further notice. The following day, the NCAA Basketball Tournament—scheduled to be held in the weeks that immediately followed—was canceled entirely. It seemed that the entire world had screeched to a halt in just a few days.

REED: Being in Florida, we hadn't yet understood the forthcoming ramifications of this disease. And as a small group of college students looking to have a good time in Florida, we decided to indulge in a popular Internet trend at the time, mixing a drink containing water, lemon juice, honey, a packet of Emergen-C vitamin C, and vodka. Thus creating the "Quarantini." Despite its clever title and healthy ingredients, the drink is honestly disgusting.

JOHN: It was a really strange experience. On the one hand, everything felt normal—we were with our friends, enjoying a trip that we'd had planned for a number of months. On the other, it seemed like the unthinkable was occurring every time I opened Twitter. The moment I realized that things would be different, at least as far as we were concerned, was when Princeton announced that its students were to return home rather than to campus following spring break. Once that went public, I had a sense that they'd forced most other universities' hands, and within the next day, we heard similar news from Father Jenkins. By the time the NCAAs had been canceled, I'd met up with my family in the Keys. Just a week prior, I never could have imagined that I'd be heading home rather than back to school, but I'm certain that most of us who experienced March 2020 have a very similar story.

As administrators, coaches, and professors scrambled to come up with a workable plan, the entire team was sent home. And though some initially planned to stay in South Bend, the Guglielmino Athletic Complex—the center of a Notre Dame football player's daily life under normal circumstances—was shut down completely, along with the rest of campus. Students were unable to get into their dorm rooms, and players accustomed to spending several hours in the facility each day couldn't even access their lockers.

JOHN: At the beginning of the school year, I'd moved to a house off campus with a few teammates. And though I'd enjoyed the freedom and flexibility it provided throughout the year, I felt very lucky to be able to return to South Bend and grab my clothes, computer, and other basic items that I knew I would need for however long I was away. I can't imagine what I would have done if I hadn't been able to do that—particularly with as long as things lasted.

REED: I lived off-campus as well. Having a house in South Bend was extremely beneficial for multiple reasons this year. My roommates and I could pick up our things at a time that worked for us, and we had a place to spend time together when quarantining at home became slightly too monotonous—to put it diplomatically.

Perhaps the only reassurance that coaches, players, and support staff had during these unprecedented times was the fact that every school across the country was in the same boat, so to speak. Most programs aren't used to having their guys away for more than a few weeks at a time, and even then players are expected to stay in shape and check in regularly with teammates and members of the coaching staff. Now, programs were forced to grapple with widely disparate conditions nationwide, monitoring the personal health of each of their athletes and coaches, as well as attempting to put together plans to return to campus in time for a fall season. Add in the fact that virtually all gyms and health clubs were closed nationwide—making it nearly impossible for many players to lift weights independently—and it becomes clear how tumultuous the months of March and April were for Notre Dame and football programs across the country. From the coaches to the strength and conditioning staff to the operations team, the program utilized all technology available to ensure the players were staying active, keeping healthy, learning the material, and staying up to date on team announcements.

JOHN: I was lucky that I had access to some weight equipment while we were in quarantine. A former high school coach of mine has a pretty nice setup in his garage, so it was nice to be able to go over there, get some exercise, and do something that felt a little bit normal during a time where nothing else really did. Coach Balis did a great job of keeping us engaged remotely—he provided us with a workout program and made himself available as a resource for any questions we had regarding exercise, nutrition, or anything else. I can only imagine how challenging it was to try to create a program for 110 guys, based all over the country and in wildly different circumstances, and he deserves a ton of credit for all he did for us during that time.

REED: I believe the program did an exceptional job keeping the players in check. I would wake up, check in with my CoachMePlus app, look for announcements on Teamworks, follow the day's workout routine on Teambuildr, and prepare for my Zoom linebackers meeting with the Learn to Win app. We may have been at home, but it was no vacation.

As the 2020 Irish sought to remain cohesive as a team from across the country, they were also challenged with the prospect of attending school remotely. Administrators had given professors an extra week following spring break to make adjustments and plans for the second half of the semester, but challenges persisted. Most classes at Notre Dame are small and include significant interaction between students and professors—something that simply doesn't happen as naturally over Zoom. It was an adjustment, and though all parties certainly did their best to adjust given the circumstances, it was a poor substitute for the on-campus experience.

As April turned to May, uncertainty continued to beset the entire sports landscape. Professional leagues were nowhere near returning, and many began to wonder about the viability of any college football season in the fall. May optimism was quickly tempered with reports of spiking caseloads in America's Sun Belt, effectively dashing any hopes for a quick recovery. As Notre Dame students finished their semester virtually, there remained significant uncertainty with regard to a fall season. As June approached and news began to trickle in that other programs were making plans to return, the 2020 Fighting Irish found themselves in something of a holding pattern. On June 2, it became official that the season opener against Navy, scheduled to be held on August 26 in Dublin, Ireland, would be moved stateside—the first official schedule change as a result of the pandemic.

> **JOHN:** Though we had figured for a while that—due to the ban on international travel as well as the trouble Europe was having with COVID-19—we wouldn't be heading to Ireland, it was still extremely disappointing to hear the news. The Mahoney name is Irish, and I was so excited to visit the Emerald Isle for the first time—as a member of the Fighting Irish, no less.

> **REED:** I always had so much respect for the history behind this yearly matchup. After the Great Depression and World War II, Notre Dame was struggling financially. To help support the university, the U.S. Navy created a training facility on Notre Dame's campus to help keep the school running. Regardless of either team's success, the teams would face each other every year out of respect. I was saddened to hear that not only would we not be traveling to Ireland but that COVID had put this tradition on hold for the year.

Around the same time, the entire nation found itself embroiled in social turmoil following the death of George Floyd, an unarmed African-American man, at the hands of the Minneapolis Police Department. Protests ensued across the nation, and many

Americans were both horrified and forced to confront issues that they had previously been oblivious to. Though the team had yet to return to campus, coaches scheduled Zoom calls to give players the opportunity to share their thoughts on what had happened, describe their past experiences, and discuss ways that their coaches, teammates, and university could become part of the solution, ultimately working toward greater social justice and tolerance.

> **JOHN:** It was certainly an eye-opening experience for someone like me. I'd never been confronted with or forced to grapple with some of these societal realities, and to hear teammates that I knew and respected tremendously tell their stories with regard to discrimination that they themselves had encountered was certainly sobering. As tough as the discussion was to have, I remember feeling very proud to be part of a team that was bold enough to address these issues head on. During the call, Coach Lea referred to us as the "future leaders of our country," and it was then that truly I realized the importance of what we were doing.

> **REED:** It was moving to hear the trials and tribulations my teammates had experienced over the years. It was the most compelling, emotional, and powerful meeting I had ever been a part of.

These efforts culminated in a Juneteenth rally, held on campus on June 19 to commemorate the anniversary of the final emancipation of slaves in the United States. Senior captain Daelin Hayes and junior offensive lineman Max Siegel addressed the attendees, along with head coach Brian Kelly and university president Father John Jenkins. Though Notre Dame's record on social issues had always been strong—particularly since Father Hesburgh's work on the Civil Rights Commission in the 1960s—this was a major step for a program and institution proud of its traditional values.

For someone like Siegel, who'd been an advocate for an enhanced societal commitment to racial and social justice since his youth, efforts like this were a long time coming. When asked about the significance of the university's public commitment to increased equality, he said, "It's something that we've been pushing for, for a long time, and I'm glad that more people are conscious of these issues. It's just unfortunate that it had to get to this point for these discussions to finally occur."

> **JOHN:** Admittedly, prior to 2020, I'd never even heard of Juneteenth. Around the time of the march, however, I did more research and learned about its historical significance. It's an incredible story, and Max really put things into perspective for me when he referred to it as "the equivalent of the Fourth of July for Black Americans." That's a profound, telling statement—and one that I found to be very thought-provoking.

For the team to even be on campus for the rally, however, there was significant planning and legwork done by the medical staff to ensure a safe return and reintegration into team activities. On June 4, the entire team gathered via Zoom to learn of the protocols and procedures by which they could return to campus. Players were sorted into three tiers, allowing for a staged return that would reduce the burden on the training staff and ensure that proper monitoring of athletes' health could occur. Furthermore, each player was to live in the Morris Inn—the hotel on campus—for the duration of the summer. There would be a forced quarantine upon arrival, and players were not allowed to spend time even with one another prior to their first test. Each player would have his own room, and meals would be delivered to his door so as to avoid contact. This promised a dull, onerous existence—but one that was absolutely necessary if there was to be a season that fall.

To start with, workouts occurred in groups of approximately 10 players to ensure adequate space for social distancing—placing a significant burden on a strength staff already forced to make significant adjustments to its standard operating procedure. Players and coaches were required to wear masks throughout the entire workout, and every piece of equipment that was touched—plates, machines, bands, or whatever else—was to be fully sanitized following its use. Furthermore, players weren't supposed to spend any unnecessary time in the already socially distanced locker room. The directive was to shower and change (while wearing masks) as quickly as possible, then leave before the next group arrived so as to minimize any potential for exposure. Pre-pandemic, it wasn't uncommon for players to spend hours in the locker room, so this was a challenge for many of them to adapt to.

JOHN: One of the biggest adjustments for me was no longer having a designated partner during my lift. It was one of my first lifts following my return to campus and, not thinking anything of it, I went to spot a teammate who was about to begin a particularly heavy set of bench press, only to be quickly and harshly informed that that wasn't something we were allowed to do anymore.

As the season drew closer, reports of shutdowns and COVID-19-related complications continued to pour in from programs across the country. Ohio State, Indiana, North Carolina, Kansas State, and a number of other programs across the Power 5 were forced to pause workouts due to outbreaks within the program. This proved challenging from an optics perspective, to be sure, as outside observers wondered publicly why college athletes were forced to return so quickly, particularly as most of society remained relatively isolated. Practically speaking, however, this was certainly problematic for these teams—who now found their preseason training completely interrupted as August and the opening of preseason camp inched closer.

Following the players' return to campus and through the months of June and July, however, the Irish were able to stay relatively healthy and unaffected. There were a few isolated cases, but nothing so serious as to force a shutdown. However, schedule adjustments made across college football nevertheless placed Notre Dame, as college football's most prominent independent, in a precarious position. On July 9, the Big Ten announced that it would be moving to a conference-only schedule, effectively canceling the highly anticipated Notre Dame–Wisconsin matchup scheduled for October 3 at Lambeau Field. The Pac-12 followed suit the next day, forcing USC and Stanford—traditional rivalries and mainstays for the Irish every year—off the schedule. Just like that, a series that had gone uninterrupted since World War II was on hiatus, and Notre Dame suddenly had three large holes in its schedule to fill.

REED: Notre Dame and USC are two schools that cherish tradition. Our teams had faced off every year since 1926, barring three years during World War II. Although it held less historical significance than our Navy rivalry, the USC game had always been praised by fans on both sides. In the past few years, particularly, both teams had been relatively dominant, and the matchups were continually full of excitement. It was disheartening to hear another annual matchup had fallen by the wayside because of the pandemic.

JOHN: Losing the Ireland game was tough, to be sure, but it was the loss of these three matchups that really made clear that this season would be different than any other. The schedule had been set up so that every game not played in South Bend—save for our trip to Ireland—would be played in an NFL stadium. There's obviously never a *good* time for something like COVID to occur, but to miss out on experiences like the ones we had planned for 2020 was a real shame.

In the weeks that followed, athletic director Jack Swarbrick and his team of administrators in South Bend maneuvered to ensure that a season could still be played despite the adjustments to the schedule. An announcement by the SEC that it too would be moving to a conference-only scheduling model removed Arkansas from the Irish schedule, leaving us with just eight games on the 2020 slate. Notre Dame's independence—which provides a tremendous benefit to the program as well as the university under normal circumstances—was threatening to leave it on college football's fringes as the landscape shifted to manage a global pandemic.

Following weeks of speculation, however, it was announced on July 29 that, for the first time in program history, Notre Dame football would play as a member of a conference. The ACC—where the majority of the Irish sports teams already competed—announced that it would be moving to a 10-game conference schedule for the 2020 season, and that Notre Dame would be included and eligible to compete for the conference championship. There were already six games scheduled between Notre Dame and ACC schools—not the least of which was a matchup with Clemson to be held November 7 in South Bend—which would minimize any additional adjustments to the schedule. With the stroke of a pen, the Irish added Syracuse, Florida State, Boston College, and North Carolina to their schedule. Furthermore, Notre Dame agreed to share the revenue from its NBC television contract with the other member schools—a major step for a school so insistent on its independence.

> **JOHN:** Given the circumstances, the move made all the sense in the world. I never got used to seeing the ACC insignia on the field, goal posts, or jerseys, but I'll always be grateful that they let us join and enabled us to have a season. We'll always be able to say that we were on the first and only Notre Dame team to ever compete in a conference, which is a factoid that I'm sure I'll be able to use at a dinner party at some point down the road.

> **REED:** In the past, Notre Dame had been criticized for being independent. Some accused the team of picking and choosing easier schedules when in all actuality, Notre Dame's schedules have been historically difficult. This year, we would prove them all wrong. That being said, I think ND Football's Twitter account said it best, commenting on a video of the ACC emblem being painted on our field, "Felt cute, might delete next year :)"

Unfortunately, as part of the scheduling arrangement, the one non-conference game that would remain on the schedule would have to be played within the state of Indiana. Since the game against the Naval Academy was to be played in Annapolis, at the Midshipmen's home stadium, it couldn't be played in 2020—snapping a streak of annual matchups that dated to 1927. The

Notre Dame–Navy rivalry is historically and institutionally significant for both schools, and though the Irish wouldn't have to prepare for Navy's vaunted triple-option offense, to have the game fall off the schedule entirely was extremely disappointing. Navy had supported Notre Dame during a challenging period during World War II, and Father Hesburgh had pledged to keep the Middies on the schedule for as long as they liked as thanks for their help. It's a bond that extends far beyond the gridiron, and the annual game is a reminder not only of the two institutions' rich histories but also Notre Dame's place in the fabric of our nation's heritage.

The uneasiness associated with joining a conference and not playing games with USC and Navy was indicative of a greater reality felt across college football—that, as the season continued to draw closer, significant and unprecedented uncertainty remained. As the student body prepared to return to campus, it became increasingly clear that this year would look and feel different than any before it.

2

THE FIRST WAVE

It was the first week of August 2020. It was characteristically muggy in South Bend, and the Fighting Irish had just finished summer workouts and were in the midst of preparing for their first conference season in school history. Earlier that summer, a revised academic calendar had been released. In the interest of creating a "bubble" on campus, the fall break had been eliminated, the semester would finish prior to Thanksgiving, and school would begin two weeks before its originally scheduled start date. Rather than travel to Ireland or Annapolis to begin the season against Navy, the Irish were now slated to open the season at home against Duke on September 12. The traditional preseason trip to Culver Academy for training camp had been canceled, and the start of practice was now scheduled to begin around the same time as the school year—forcing the coaching staff to adjust its preparation schedule.

> **JOHN:** Traditionally, camp is the most grueling part of our year. There are no school commitments to worry about, and the NCAA eases up on the 20-hour weekly restriction, so it's all football, all day. It's a grind, but a team really establishes its identity during those few weeks. I was curious to see how things would work under these different circumstances.

REED: I was personally relieved to have class during camp this year. It meant that there would be some form of break between practice sessions. In past years, camp was a nonstop football marathon. Whether it was practice, workouts or meetings, days were filled to the brim with football activities.

Obviously, a return to in-person academics necessarily involved the return of the student body, which presented significant issues from a COVID-19 perspective. Keeping 100 players in a hotel healthy and free from infection was challenging enough. Adding 12,000 young adults to that equation—many of whom hadn't seen their friends since March and were eager to return to campus and be social—promised to make a difficult situation borderline untenable.

Across the country, college football's prospects for a fall season appeared to dim considerably each day. The Ivy League—the first conference to cancel sporting events at the pandemic's inception—had canceled its season in mid-July, and on August 5, UConn became the first FBS program to cancel its 2020 season. In the days that followed, speculation continued to mount as rumors about the Big Ten, Pac-12, and other conferences continued to swirl. On August 8, the MAC announced that it would be canceling its season, and reports arose that the Big Ten Presidents' meeting the following day would likely result in a similar outcome.

JOHN: August 8 was a Saturday, and some of us were actually out on the golf course as all the news seemed to intensify. It was truly a surreal experience—you'd check your phone after each hole and things would appear to have gotten worse. After all the measures that had been taken to try to make things work, it seemed like our hopes for a season were all but gone. It was an extremely powerless feeling.

The following day, however, the #WeWantToPlay movement—backed and promoted by stars such as Clemson quarterback Trevor Lawrence and Ohio State quarterback Justin Fields, among many others—began to spread across social media. It was a degree of personal advocacy that college sports fans weren't used to seeing from their athletes, and it had a substantial impact on the public opinion surrounding the 2020 season. No longer were players seen simply as pawns in the machine's desire for profit. Instead, the world began to realize that they were willing to make the necessary sacrifices to be able to compete.

Despite the display of support for a fall season on social media, however, things continued to move in the opposite direction. On August 10, the Mountain West Conference announced its plans to cancel. The next day, the Big Ten and Pac-12 formally followed suit, leaving the ACC, SEC, and Big 12 as the only Power 5 conferences still open to playing a fall season. Each released public statements affirming its commitment to playing, but if the past weeks and months had shown anything, it was that those plans could change quickly.

Amidst the turmoil, classes and practice began on campus in South Bend. As students adjusted to a life of near-constant mask wearing and social distancing, the team began to practice. With the added challenge of classwork with preseason camp, it was a grind for the first few weeks. The coaching staff was resilient in its efforts to reproduce a relatively camp-like atmosphere. The practices were long, and the nights were hot. Although the team had an extremely strenuous summer workout program, the players were visibly less conditioned due to unavoidable COVID restrictions.

Faced with a difficult, if not impossible situation, coaches tried their best not to sound contradictory. They needed the players to social distance and stay safe, but also wanted the players at the Gug, training and learning scheme.

JOHN: On the first day of class, I was introduced to the unfortunate reality of contact tracing. Though I'd tested negative that morning, I was deemed to be a "close contact" of an individual that tested positive, forcing me to isolate for the better part of two weeks. It was something that many people had to deal with at one time or another, but it was a tremendous disappointment—particularly since it forced me to miss two weeks of practice as the season was just beginning.

REED: These were a particularly tough two weeks for me. John and the rest of his house—the majority of walk-on seniors—were contact traced. I had to carry on without my closest friends on the team and fellow signalers. In a non-pandemic year, all three signalers, John, Pat Pelini, and I, would meet in the locker room before meetings and create signals for the new calls Coach Lea had sent us. This year, I was forced to be especially creative. Defensive analyst Nick Lezynski would hand me the call sheet for practice. I would scan through it for the new calls. If I had enough time, I would text Pat and John to see if they had any suggestions for the new calls, but on several occasions that week, I had to come up with signals on the spot. During the defensive unit meetings, I would stand at the front of the auditorium and perform the signals as Coach Lea read aloud the new calls. With over 200 different calls, some signals were bound to be met with some backlash for appearing too similar to another and would have to go back to the drawing board. On top of this, opposing teams stealing hand signals had become increasingly more common over the past few years. Coach Lea wanted us to create multiple signals for the same call and ensure the players knew them. I remember FaceTiming John and Pat minutes before meetings, wailing my arms around trying to find something that could be even slightly conceivable as the new call. Suffice it to say, I was overjoyed when the "WOPU" house was allowed to return.

Following an arduous first week, the pandemic began to intensify on campus. Testing results from August 17 and 18 returned 104 and 95 positive tests, respectively, forcing university administrators to move classes entirely online for two weeks. Though the football team remained relatively unaffected, it was nevertheless forced to pause practices and workouts due to the campus-wide shutdown. In his address to the student body, Father Jenkins pleaded with students to exercise caution and adhere to social-distancing practices, making clear that if case numbers did not return to a manageable range in the near future, he would have no choice but to send students home for the semester—which would undoubtedly create additional uncertainty about playing football that fall.

Across the country, fellow ACC member North Carolina announced that all undergraduate classes would be moved online—casting further doubt over the feasibility of a fall season and raising challenging questions about the logistics of in-person college sports in the absence of in-person college. Was it right to keep athletes on campus while regular students were forced to return home? And if so, what does that say about the athletes' relationship with the university, since there is clearly more being asked of them than regular students? These questions arose at a time when calls to compensate college athletes had grown louder, placing university administrators, coaches, and the NCAA in a difficult position.

Amid the turmoil, however, life continued on in South Bend. Despite having to attend class virtually, the team returned to practice after a brief shutdown. Face coverings were required, and the training staff was incredibly vigilant about enforcing distancing on the sidelines. Though the team had stayed relatively healthy amid the chaos on campus, there were inevitably a few isolated cases—made worse by contact tracing, since infected players' close contacts were predominantly their teammates.

JOHN: Since those of us who had been traced had missed the first week of practice, we were required to rejoin the team while adhering to the NCAA's rules about acclimatization. This meant that we could only wear helmets for the first two days, transition to shells for the next two days, then finally pad up fully on the fifth day. This was a pain, to be sure, but even more painful was the return to intense practices after two weeks of what amounted to forced inactivity. I could hardly make it through individual drills those first couple of days back, and it took a while to get my wind and legs back. As much as I wanted to believe they would, push-ups and sit-ups in my bedroom couldn't keep me in shape—and I can't imagine that I was the only guy, at Notre Dame or across the country, who ran into this issue.

As the Kentucky Derby—postponed from its usual slot on the first Saturday in May—was held at Churchill Downs, the college football season opened in earnest with a BYU-Navy matchup over Labor Day weekend. The Cougars won convincingly—a sign, perhaps, of what they had planned for the rest of the season—and college football fans were given a taste of normalcy in a year that had sorely lacked it. Then, once Tuesday rolled around, it was game week in South Bend. The two-week shutdown was over, school was back in session, and the team's routine began to feel slightly normal. As Attitude Tuesday turned to Grit Wednesday, the team was confident and extremely excited to finally take the field.

All things considered, it was an ideal opener for the Irish. Playing at home is always an advantage, and the administration had announced in late August that only students, faculty, and staff, along with players' families, would be able to attend games that fall. The entire crowd would be masked, and an elaborate plan created by a Notre Dame data analytics professor would, at least in theory, ensure social distancing in the crowd from the opening kick through the final whistle. Though this limited Notre Dame Stadium to less than 20 percent of its stated capacity of 77,622, it would still provide a distinct home-field advantage— which, as many programs across the country prepared to play in front of entirely empty stadiums, was significant. The Blue Devils are always a well-coached team—their head coach, David Cutcliffe, is known as one of Peyton Manning's mentors—but the Irish had defeated them handily in Durham the year before. And though Duke had added Clemson transfer Chase Brice at quarter-back, the Irish had a clear advantage from a talent perspective. It was a quality opponent, to be sure, but Notre Dame would most likely have a decent margin for error throughout. According to the Vegas oddsmakers, the Irish were 20-point favorites—indicating a clear advantage for the home team.

Following Friday's walk-through, the team headed to the DoubleTree in Downtown South Bend—its usual spot the night prior to home games. There was no pep rally this year, nor would there be the customary player walk across campus before the game the next day. Parents weren't allowed in the hotel before the game, either, so the focus was entirely on the task at hand. In the socially distanced meeting rooms before the game, players watched film and went over their assignments once more before heading to their rooms for the night.

> **JOHN:** There were a fair number of new calls in that week, so the signalers got together to make a video that went over some of the trickier ones so the guys could prep that night. Things ran smoothly the next day, so I was glad we did it.

> **REED:** It was not only our job to create the hand signals, but to make sure all the players knew the signals and would be able to recognize them from the field. The videos were immensely helpful in our endeavors, so we sent them in every position's group chat.

Following the walk-through the next morning—which occurred on the turf at the former College Football Hall of Fame across the street—the team ate lunch and boarded buses to head to the stadium. Rather than go to the Gug for a final team meeting, we pulled up directly in front of the north gate, and the players entered the stadium to prepare for the first conference game in program history. There was no shortage of speculation about how this season's unique scheduling arrangement would impact Notre Dame and college football as a whole. That morning, on ESPN's *College GameDay,* analysts Desmond Howard and David Pollack agreed that the Irish schedule—and likelihood of making the playoff—was set up more favorably following their entry into the ACC. And though it may have seemed that way on paper, the fact remained that it still needed to be proven on the field. We'd have 11 opportunities to do so that season, and the first was that afternoon.

Once the team entered the locker room, however, pregame proceeded as it normally did. The defensive players set down their bags, went down the tunnel, and met on the 50-yard-line for a pregame prayer and Coach Lea's final thoughts. They then returned to the locker room to tape, dress, and prepare for warmups—which began for the kickers and punters 68 minutes before kickoff. By position group, the rest of the team trickled out to join them, giving a largely empty stadium its first glimpse of the 2020 Fighting Irish.

With 24 minutes left on the pregame clock, the Irish punt team aligned on the goal line. Punter Jay Bramblett booted to Lawrence Keys III, and the entire team gathered on the field prior to returning to the locker room. They broke down on Coach Kelly, then headed back up the tunnel to rehydrate and make a few final adjustments prior to kickoff. After a 15-minute break, Kelly addressed the team—reminding the players of all they'd gone through to get to that point and reminding them of their opportunity to make history that afternoon. Throughout Notre Dame's storied history—one that included 11 national championships, 22 undefeated regular seasons, and more than 900 total wins—they'd never won a conference game. With an 18-game home winning streak on the line, the 2020 Irish had the chance to do that—and make the first mark in the chapter they hoped to themselves write in the Notre Dame history books. Following Coach Kelly's speech, the team gathered to pray—as they always do before games, home or away. After slapping the PLAY LIKE A CHAMPION TODAY sign, the team gathered in the tunnel for a few moments prior to taking the field. Upon Mike Collins's iconic "Here Come the Irish" declaration over the loudspeaker, the team took a completely empty field. Thanks to the

COVID-related restrictions, there was no band or cheer squad, as there might have been under normal circumstances.

> **JOHN:** As we gathered in the tunnel before taking the field, I couldn't help but think about all the adversity that we, as well as our university and society more generally, had overcome just to get to that point. Though it certainly didn't feel normal, we got to play that day—with our parents, friends, and classmates in the stands watching us. We had a lot to be thankful for, and I resolved to not take a minute of it for granted.

> **REED:** Running out of the tunnel onto the field was no less satisfying than any other year. Yes, there were fewer fans in the stands, and there was no band or cheerleaders on the field, but it is still one of the best feelings in the world. We had gone through so much to get here, and this moment had made it all worth it.

As kickoff neared, fifth-year-senior quarterback Ian Book walked alone to midfield to represent the Irish at the opening coin toss. This was another COVID adjustment; rather than send four captains to midfield, as is tradition, it was deemed safer to send just one player. The Blue Devils won the toss and elected to receive, which sent senior kicker Jon Doerer and the Irish kickoff team onto the field to start Notre Dame's 2020 campaign—the 133rd in school history. After a booming kick, Jeremiah Owusu-Koramoah laid a crushing blow on the returner inside the Duke 20, forcing the Blue Devils to begin their opening drive at their own 16. The crowd exploded, and the socially distanced band began to play. For all the strangeness that 2020 had brought, there was suddenly a refreshing hint of normalcy for all those watching in person and on TV.

On the first snap, however, Brice found tight end Noah Gray in the flat. He rumbled for a gain of 22, making clear that the Blue Devils had no qualms about potentially ruining Notre Dame's conference debut. Then, on second-and-7, a 12-yard carry brought Duke into Irish territory. From there, however, the Irish defense bowed up, forcing a turnover on downs keyed by a fourth-and-2 pass deflection by safety Kyle Hamilton. Book and the offense took the ball at their own 39, set on striking first.

JOHN: One of Coach Lea's fundamental philosophies is that of "Head, body, head, body." It comes from *The Fighter*, the Mark Wahlberg movie about "Irish" Micky Ward—a former welterweight boxing champ. At its core, it's about taking punches (or, in our case, absorbing big plays) while remaining competitive, allowing you to stay in a game when things may not be going your way. In this day and age, offenses in college football are good enough that allowing explosive plays from time to time is inevitable. The best defenses are the ones that can quickly respond and recover, and this drive was the first opportunity we had to display our ability to do that. This resilience became part of our identity as the year progressed, and it began right then.

Unfortunately, the Irish offense was unable to capitalize on its good starting field position, as it was forced to punt following a three-and-out. The Irish special teams units continued their strong start, as a 52-yard punt from Bramblett put the Blue Devils on a long field once more. Much like the previous drive, the Duke offense tallied two quick first downs, after which its drive began to stall. On third-and-5 from the Duke 37, the Irish brought pressure, hoping to force a punt and get off the field. As is often the case, though, the blitzing linebackers left enough space over the middle for Brice to find Eli Pancol on a rub route just shy of the sticks. From there, he broke tackles and raced downfield until cornerback TaRiq Bracy made a touchdown-saving tackle at the Irish 8. The 55-yard catch-and-run again had the Irish defense on its heels as the Blue Devils suddenly threatened to jump out to an early lead.

Just as on the previous drive, however, the Irish defense dug in. After a Kurt Hinish tackle for loss on first down, Duke was unable to move the ball any closer—forcing a 29-yard field-goal attempt on fourth-and-goal from the 11. Kicker Charlie Ham connected, and Duke took an early 3–0 lead. Despite the fact that it had surrendered some big plays, things could have been a lot worse for the Notre Dame defense. It had found itself in a couple tough spots and had, for the most part, escaped—allowing just three points on the first two drives. With seven minutes to play in the first quarter, it was the offense's turn to contribute.

The second drive for the Irish got off to a promising start, as freshman running back Chris Tyree returned the kickoff 38 yards in his first collegiate touch. Displaying the speed he was renowned for in high school, he showed impressive toughness for a young player—hitting the hole without hesitation and carrying a Blue Devils tackler five yards before going to the ground.

JOHN: From the instant that you saw that kid touch the ball in practice, it was clear he was going to be special. He just moves faster than everyone else, and he was a much more mature ball carrier than I would have expected for a freshman.

Despite the strong opener, the Irish offense was unable to sustain any momentum, going three-and-out and punting to the Blue Devils from their own 39. Duke found a similar amount of success on its ensuing drive, mustering one first down before a second-down holding penalty set their offense too far behind the chains to keep its hopes of extending its lead alive. However, a 60-yard punt from Porter Wilson flipped the field, placing the Irish on their own 19 with just over three minutes to play in the first quarter. From there, the teams traded punts once more, and as the first quarter waned, it appeared that Notre Dame's ACC debut was shaping up to be a defensive struggle.

> **JOHN:** We'd settled in defensively, and you could feel the unit's confidence growing with every tackle, incompletion, and third-down stop. The first-game jitters had evaporated, and coaches and players alike were happy with the execution on the two most recent drives.

Another excellent punt from Porter Wilson stuck the Irish on their own 4 as they began their fourth drive. A completion to tight end Tommy Tremble moved the chains on third down for the first Irish first down of the day, but two incompletions on the next series left Notre Dame with yet another fourth down deep in its own territory. After another disappointing drive, it appeared that the Irish would again be forced to punt. Bramblett and the punt team took the field, but rather than punt, he took the snap around the left end and found a cutback lane that gave him enough room to gain a first down and extend the Irish drive. Rather than send the defense back onto the field, Kelly could stick with his offense, which now had a first-and-10 from the 35.

> **JOHN:** All week in practice, Coach Polian had told us that we'd run the fake if we got the look we wanted. Clearly, we did, and it was the spark we needed to get things going offensively. It's

a risky move that deep in your own territory, but Jay is a really good athlete—much better than people give him credit for—and we were confident he could make it work for us.

REED: Outside of punting, Jay Bramblett was a respectable quarterback in high school. I would often throw deep passes with him before practices and was always surprised by his strength. He had a strong arm and felt very comfortable with the ball in hands. The perfect set of skills for a punter to have. It allows for a variety of fake-punt opportunities and keeps the other team on its toes.

Following the first down, Book wasted no time—finding freshman tight end Michael Mayer for a 17-yard gain that brought the Irish past midfield. A first-down carry by Kyren Williams moved them even further, and a face-mask penalty against the Blue Devils placed them on the Duke 22. They gained 20 more on a perfectly executed screen pass to senior Jafar Armstrong, and Kyren Williams capped the Irish drive with a hard-fought touchdown carry soon thereafter. Notre Dame had its first lead of the game, and a Doerer extra point made it 7–3 with 10:39 to play in the first half.

From there, the Blue Devils offense went three-and-out, but the Irish offense was unable to keep its momentum from the prior drive—punting from around midfield to give Brice and the Duke offense another long field. They moved the ball efficiently, getting as far as the Notre Dame 2 before an Isaiah Foskey sack on third down forced another field-goal attempt. From 30 yards out, Ham connected once again to cut the Blue Devils deficit to a single point.

REED: Isaiah Foskey had been turning heads since the first time he stepped on Notre Dame's campus, a wholesome guy who was truly in his element his second year on the team. Throughout the season, he was uniquely valuable and productive in our third-down "penny" package.

Notre Dame regained possession with 3:15 to play in the first half, knowing that it needed to score points before heading to the locker room for halftime. Offensive coordinator Tommy Rees called a tunnel screen on first down, and Williams found space down the sideline. He was chased down after a 75-yard gain, and the Irish suddenly found themselves just 11 yards from paydirt. On the next play, however, Book threw an interception, overshooting Tommy Tremble over the middle. An opportunity to take control of the game had been squandered, and the Irish defense was forced back onto the field to protect the team's one-point lead.

JOHN: After the big play, it felt like we were about ready to break the game open. Red zone turnovers are always unfortunate, but that one stung. Over the headset, Coach Lea reiterated the importance of the coming drive for our defense, urging the unit to respond to this adversity with the toughness and discipline it had shown all day.

Following a 15-yard completion on first down, the Duke offense again stalled. A punt from the Blue Devils' own 41 gave the Irish one more chance before halftime, though they had just over a minute to rectify the poor ending to the previous drive. Three completions to junior Joe Wilkins Jr. got the Irish into field-goal range with a few seconds left, and Doerer stayed perfect from 48 yards out to make it 10–6 as the teams headed in for halftime.

In the Notre Dame locker room, the emphasis was on cleaning up the mistakes made in the first half. Following its slow start, the offense had shown flashes of dominance but had missed too many opportunities to take control. The defense had looked strong and only allowed six points—but had allowed 12 first downs, giving the Blue Devils too much control. The Irish were slated to receive the opening kick, giving them an opportunity to take the game over immediately, as Coach Kelly urged them to before returning to the field.

Following a 10-yard run on first down, however, the drive stalled, forcing Bramblett and the punt team back onto the field. There was no trickery this time, and he punted to the Duke 36. On third down, Brice found a receiver on a slant over the middle, and it appeared that they would again move the chains. Owusu-Koramoah, however, had other plans—raking the ball out and forcing a fumble that was recovered by Shaun Crawford at the Notre Dame 41. The defense had again come through, giving the offense the ball on a short field with the opportunity to take a two-score lead.

> **JOHN:** Coach Lea preaches "ball disruption," and plays like that are the reason why. Turnovers are critical in close games like that, and Wu made an outstanding play to swing the momentum back in our direction.

This time around, Book and the Irish offense would not be denied. On a fourth-and-1 from the Duke 26, Williams went untouched around the left end for a long-awaited Notre Dame touchdown—his second of the afternoon. The Doerer extra point sailed through the uprights, and the Irish now held an 11-point lead.

From there, they traded punts again. A short kick from Bramblett deep in his own territory put the Blue Devils on a short field, however, and consecutive first-down completions from Brice had Duke within striking distance. A designed quarterback run on third-and-goal from the 2 was successful, and the Blue Devils found the end zone for the first time that day. The extra point was good, and with 2:19 to play, the score was 17–13. It was clear that, despite the 20-point spread, this one would be a four-quarter battle.

Luckily for the Irish, however, the offense put together their best drive of the day soon thereafter—a 15-play masterpiece that featured four third-down conversions and took more than six minutes off the clock. A 17-yard touchdown strike from Book to senior receiver Avery Davis was the exclamation point, and with just under 11 minutes to play, the Irish led 24–13. At a critical moment, they had once again wrested control of the game away from a resilient, tough Duke team.

On the ensuing drive, the defense caused three consecutive negative plays, stifling any effort by the Blue Devils to claw back into the game. After another Duke punt, the freshman class took over for the Irish—a 25-yard carry by Tyree followed by a 14-yard grab by Mayer moved Notre Dame into the red zone, where a 34-yard Doerer field goal extended the lead to 14. And though a 23-yard third-down scramble by Brice briefly kept the Blue Devils' hopes alive, another forced fumble by Owusu-Koramoah allowed the Irish to regain possession, effectively ending things with 2:51 to play. Four Jahmir Smith carries chewed up the rest of the clock, and the game ended 27–13—moving the Irish to 1–0. It had been a solid, though unremarkable win. But, given the circumstances, Notre Dame left the field happy.

JOHN: That certainly wasn't a game where we left the stadium and felt great about our performance, but being there in the first place was a victory in its own right. We knew we had a lot to improve on, but after all we'd sacrificed just to get to that point, there wasn't much to complain about. It's certainly a truism, but a win is a win—and in 2020, you took them wherever you could get them.

Upon their return to the locker room, Coach Kelly congratulated the players on the victory—which, he reminded them, was the 19th straight at Notre Dame Stadium—as well as the first conference win in school history. He reinforced the point that there was a lot to work on, and urged the team to stay healthy and focused that evening and through the weekend. The game ball was awarded to Kyren Williams, who'd recorded more than 200 all-purpose yards and paced the Irish attack all afternoon with two touchdowns. After he led them in the fight song, the players showered, gathered their things, and left the locker room.

In a normal year, throngs of autograph seekers and rowdy tailgaters await the players as they leave the stadium to find their friends and family. This year, with the almost complete absence of fans, there was no such ruckus. For a campus that abounds with energy following a victory, it felt uncomfortably sterile.

REED: Obviously, fans used to flock to John and me after games asking for autographs and pictures, so the slight change of pace was very relaxing. Joking aside, it was odd walking through campus after a win without the constant cheer and commotion of the families, students, and alumni. At that point, my only hope was that the customary game-day atmosphere would return as the season progressed.

JOHN: It was so strange. In the past, we'd often go to our parents' tailgate and relax for a while following the game. Obviously, that wasn't allowed this year, so we went back to their hotel room and hung out there. I was glad to be able to see them, of course, but there was this inescapable sense of disappointment that I think everyone on campus felt that day. It was a football Saturday unlike any we'd experienced before.

Unfortunately, that was the nature of the world in September 2020. The pandemic raged on, and all the Irish could do was turn their focus to the next week's challenge. On the docket for the following Saturday was a home game against the only out-of-conference opponent on the schedule—the Bulls of South Florida.

CHAPTER 3

RUNNING OF THE BULLS

Following their victory over the Blue Devils, the Irish turned their focus to their only nonconference opponent of the regular season: the South Florida Bulls. Under first-year head coach Jeff Scott—a longtime Clemson assistant—they entered the game 1–0 thanks to a 27–6 victory against The Citadel the week prior. USF, a program that began play in 1997, isn't a squad that the Irish have encountered very many times throughout their history, and thus the narratives leading into Notre Dame's second home game of the season fell primarily into two categories: moving to 2–0 and avenging a painful 2011 loss to a Skip Holtz–led USF team. Though there wasn't a player on the roster around for the 2011 loss, the Irish were nevertheless eager to exorcise the demons of the past as they entered Week 2.

Anyone who's been around football can tell you that an opponent that has a new coach and is implementing a new system is always challenging to prepare for—particularly early in the season. The Bulls hadn't even been on the schedule a month earlier, so the Irish entered this matchup with a significant amount of uncertainty—anathema to a program that prides itself on exhaustive preparation. However, they knew there was one thing they'd certainly have to be ready for: speed. Weis's offenses at Florida Atlantic had been renowned for their explosiveness, and any roster composed primarily of Florida natives is almost certain to have some burners. With this in mind, and though it undoubtedly had a decided advantage in the trenches, the Notre Dame defense knew it was in for a challenge.

JOHN: Usually, the schedules are set years in advance—it's not uncommon for some of our games to be scheduled more than 10 years ahead of time. The morning of our Michigan game in 2019, it was announced that we'd be playing the Wolverines next in 2033—meaning that the seniors who will be playing in that game were second graders at the time of its announcement. Obviously, the COVID situation forced teams to be a little more flexible, but we didn't even know we'd be playing these guys until camp had already started. Given that, as well as the fact that they had an entirely new staff, there was a lot of uncertainty. It was definitely a different experience than what we're used to.

REED: Newly scheduled games were always a little underwhelming. I remember seeing the news that Notre Dame and Alabama had scheduled games, only to dig deeper and realize the games were not until 2028 and 2029. If we learned anything from this season, it's that games don't need to be scheduled that far in advance. Our team was thrown into the ACC for the first time and had a full schedule days later.

In addition, coaches and players alike felt that there was significant room for improvement following the first game. A team learns a lot about itself between its first and second game, and Coach Kelly challenged the team to focus on its development during this week of practice. The practice schedule reflected this. Attitude Tuesday and Grit Wednesday, which are usually pretty demanding under normal circumstances, were particularly grueling. For the team to achieve all that the staff knew it could in November, December, and beyond, it had to take advantage of the opportunities it had now.

As the Irish made their final preparations and headed to the team hotel on Friday night, with the country already reeling from the ongoing coronavirus crisis and just weeks away from perhaps the most contentious presidential election in recent history, was dealt shocking news that was as relevant in South Bend as it was Washington, D.C. On the evening of September 18, it was reported that Supreme Court Justice Ruth Bader Ginsburg, an American icon, had passed away—leaving a vacancy on the nation's highest court less than two months before President Trump sought reelection. Soon thereafter, speculation began to mount that Trump would seek to nominate Amy Coney Barrett—a Notre Dame alum and law professor—for the vacancy.

> **JOHN:** I'm the first to acknowledge that it is cliché to talk about remembering "where you were" when a significant historical event occurs, but I can honestly say that I'll never forget learning of this news. In the past, they had traveled all the signalers to the hotel prior to home games, but—in the interest of minimizing exposure and reducing the size of the travel party—they decided before this game to only bring one. Reed was chosen to make the trip, which gave me the freedom to grab dinner with some of the freshmen—who were predictably having a tough time adjusting to life on campus given all the restrictions. I was halfway through a plate of wings when I checked my phone and saw the news. Obviously, the passing of someone like Justice Ginsburg is tragic, regardless of circumstance. As if 2020 hadn't already been challenging enough, the thought of the nation having to go through something like this, as it dealt with so much already, certainly

gave me pause. Having followed the confirmation process for Justice Kavanaugh just two years prior, however, I figured that Judge Barrett would be on the short list of candidates. I'd seen her and her family at Mass before, and I soon learned that they lived just a couple blocks away from me in my neighborhood just south of campus. South Bend had already found itself in the spotlight politically this year with Mayor Pete Buttigieg's run for president, and it was almost surreal to think that so much national attention would again fall on our community.

On a sunny September Saturday, however, very few of the 10,085 present at Notre Dame Stadium were concerned with politics or the federal judiciary. The student body—allowed to attend the games and a couple weeks removed from a two-week hiatus on in-person class attendance—was out in full force. Though the pandemic still raged across the country, there was a prevailing sense on campus that the worst was behind them. Following the outbreak at the beginning of the school year, case numbers had dropped, and things were starting to feel slightly more normal. It was sunny and 62 degrees—absolutely ideal conditions for a game in South Bend.

Once the game began, it became clear that any concerns the Irish had about the Bulls were of little consequence. Following a poor opening kick from South Florida, the offense began at its own 46-yard-line. Seven plays later, Ian Book ran four yards for an Irish touchdown, and the rout was on. Notre Dame scored on each of its next three drives, and another Ian Book rushing touchdown following a disastrous Bulls punt gave Notre Dame a 35–0 lead heading into halftime. It had been a dominant effort in the first half—just as Coach Kelly had demanded before the game—and the team had a lot to be proud of. The offense had moved the ball seemingly at will, while the defense had allowed just one first down. The Irish had outgained the Bulls 279 to 50, and there were some stellar individual performances from players the team knew it would need to count on later on in the season. Book had scored three touchdowns with his feet, while highly touted freshman Chris Tyree found paydirt for the first time in his college career.

As the team prepared to return to the field for the second half, Coach Kelly addressed the team with a promise. A stop and a score, he said, and he'd begin to substitute, with the goal of getting guys in the game who don't usually get the chance to play. In the Schivarelli recruiting lounge—where much of the non-travel squad was forced to dress due to COVID-related occupancy limitations—this was exciting news. For a group of guys accustomed to practicing more than they played, the mere hope of making it on the field generated considerable enthusiasm.

JOHN: We've had games in the past where, during the week, the coaches made reference to the possibility of getting the reserves some playing time. This wasn't one of those times, so to hear this news at halftime was a pleasant surprise. My aunt and uncle had flown in from Seattle to watch the game, and I knew how much they would enjoy getting to see my friends and me on the field. Obviously, we had to take care of business first, but I was optimistic.

REED: As a linebacker on one of the deepest linebacker cores Notre Dame had ever seen, I knew getting any time on defense was next to impossible—especially when I was one of the players who had to signal to the defense. When Coach Kelly hinted at the possibility of playing walk-ons on special teams, I was ecstatic, but forced myself to calm down and not get my hopes too high. We had been in situations before where it was possible, but didn't play out.

Following a USF penalty on the opening kickoff, the second half began with two consecutive first down completions by the Bulls—a less-than-ideal start for a Notre Dame team hoping to continue its first-half dominance. And though the Irish defense ultimately settled in and forced a turnover on downs, it wasn't before the USF offense mustered two more first downs and took more than five minutes off the clock. This was bad news for the guys on the sideline who hoped to get in the game later on, and they hoped for a quick score as Book led the offense back onto the field.

The drive got off to a fast start, as Tyree took a jet sweep around the left end for a gain of 15 on first down. On the ensuing series, a fourth-down conversion by Kyren Williams kept the drive alive, bringing the Irish to the USF 35. From there, Book found Tommy Tremble on a wheel route down the left sideline for what was initially called an incompletion but, upon further review, was determined to be a valid catch. The 27-yard pitch-and-catch moved Notre Dame to the USF 8, and another touchdown appeared to be well within its reach. With goal-to-go, however, Book was unable to connect with either Brock Wright or Joe Wilkins, and the Irish were forced to kick a field goal on fourth-and-goal from the Bulls 4. Doerer connected from 22 yards out, and the Irish extended their lead to 38 with 6:34 to play in the third quarter. They were taking care of business, but there was no denying that they'd opened the second half more sloppily than they'd planned to.

REED: Standing on the sideline casually, in full green pinny, hat, and headset, I conversed with the linebackers about the upcoming drive. Suddenly, I heard the voice I had come to begrudge over the past few years shout the one thing I had hoped it would: "Gregory!" I quickly focused my eyes on Coach Polian, who stared right back at me. I ripped off my headset and pinny, handed them to whomever was next to me. I had no idea who it was—it didn't matter. I ran to the telephone table, grabbed my helmet, and sprinted to the kickoff huddle. As I raised my helmet to place it on my head, Dan, one of our equipment managers, picked the hat off my head, which I had forgotten to remove. Coach Polian told me that I was going in at the five position, taking the place of Botelho—our best kickoff player. As Doerer began his kickoff approach, I followed closely behind, ensuring I would not be offside. As I ran my heart out down the field, I realized I was about to be double-teamed. USF had not realized Botelho had been subbed out and made the adjustment. I shed one blocker, only to run directly into another, giving the first blocker time to catch up. Together, they hammered me into the ground and jumped on top of me. Not quite the Rudy story. I popped up from the turf, smiled, and ran back to the sideline. I caught Coach Kelly's eye. He smiled and jokingly said, "They knew you were dangerous." I grinned and shrugged my shoulders. I didn't care how the play ended. I had stepped foot on the field during an official game and accomplished one of my life's goals.

On the ensuing drive, the Bulls again got off to a quick start—recording two first downs in their first three plays from scrimmage. In their own territory for just the third time that game, the Irish defense buckled down, getting off the field thanks to a sack from German import Alexander Ehrensberger in his first collegiate action. It wasn't over for Notre Dame's freshman defensive ends, however, as Jordan Botelho—who had been abusing South Florida's punt team all afternoon—recovered an Osita Ekwonu–blocked punt and ran for a touchdown. Following a slow start to the second half, the Irish had reasserted their dominance and now led 45–0.

> **JOHN:** Botelho is an unbelievable talent, and it was awesome to be able to watch him put on a show that afternoon. However, he can be a bit excitable at times, and it's funny—following a brief moment of excitement after the punt was blocked, Coach Lea immediately expressed concern about what Jordan might do once he found the end zone. "Please, just don't spike it," he urged, though it was obviously beyond his control at that point. Rather than spike it, he ultimately spun the ball and avoided a 15-yard penalty, so everything ended up turning out okay.

After the touchdown, the teams traded punts as the Irish began to substitute more liberally. The third quarter ended with the score still 45–0, and though the Bulls found the red zone soon thereafter for the first time that evening, their drive again ended with a turnover on downs—preserving the shutout. Following an Irish punt and another USF turnover on downs, C'Bo Flemister and Jafar Armstrong stampeded down the field, allowing Notre Dame to score a touchdown without throwing the ball once. Set to kick off with 2:15 to play, special teams coordinator Brian Polian deployed what he later called his "Ivy League kickoff squad." Led by Brown transfer Dawson Goepferich, it featured a number of walk-ons who didn't often hear their number called on Saturdays.

JOHN: I saw the ball kicked to my side and got so excited that I overran the play. Ultimately, as I attempted to turn the corner, Reed and I ran into each other. In hindsight, it wasn't my proudest moment on a football field, but it really was such a thrill just to be out there in the first place.

REED: This time, I wanted to make an impact. I sprinted downfield and evaded one defender. With the ball carrier in sight, I turned to cut him off but overshot him. I remember getting tripped up only to realize John and I had collided. A fitting end to the game for your two favorite walk-ons. I suddenly realized that every signaler had been out on the field, and no one was prepared to signal for the defense. As I ran toward the sideline, I saw that Bo Bauer had strapped on the red pinny and headset. As I passed by him, he said, "Reed, I got this!" Although the immediacy wasn't quite there, he did a great job until one of us was ready to relieve him of his duties.

Following the kickoff, the Bulls ran the ball three times for little gain, running the clock out and closing the book on a 52–0 victory for the Irish. They had done what Coach Kelly had challenged them to do the entire week—dominate an overmatched opponent and use this game as an opportunity for development as the team headed into the heart of its schedule. Amid the excitement, Kelly reminded the team that, despite its dominance that afternoon, there wouldn't be another opponent like this on the schedule. From there on out, it was all ACC opponents. For the first time in program history, Notre Dame would test itself with a full conference slate.

Awaiting the Irish the following week were the Demon Deacons of Wake Forest. It would be their first time away from the comforts of Notre Dame Stadium, and it was common knowledge that the Deacs were a much better team than their 0–2 record indicated. It would be a challenge, no doubt—but one that the Irish were eager for. After an irregular summer and early fall, the team was getting used to a weekly routine, and things were once again starting to feel normal from a football perspective. In the locker room that afternoon, nobody could have imagined all that was to follow in the days and weeks to come.

CHAPTER 4

LIFE IN THE BUBBLE

On the morning of September 22, 2020, the Tuesday of Wake Forest week, the Irish awoke to a worrying Teamworks notification. The typical practice schedule had been canceled. The beginning of the school year was abruptly followed by a surge in positive student cases. On August 17, there were 104 positive COVID-19 tests, 95 the next day, and 85 the day after. The football team was relatively confident that if it could make it through those first few weeks with minimal positives, it could make it through the season. Unfortunately, testing didn't quite go according to plan. Following the home victory against USF, the team had more than 30 positive tests. Shortly after that week's test results came back, the Wake Forest game was canceled, and all the facilities were locked tight.

> **JOHN:** We just kept hearing about more and more guys testing positive, so as time passed, we couldn't help but wonder about the feasibility of playing that Saturday. Once we knew for sure that we wouldn't be traveling to Winston-Salem, however, we began to speculate about when, or *if*, we'd be playing again.

For the first time in a while, the players had a free schedule. A regular fall day would require the players at the facilities from 1:45 to around 8:00 PM. Now, players were forced to quarantine at home. The week after the Wake Forest game was supposed to be a bye week. Now the team faced two consecutive weeks without an opponent.

Eventually, enough time passed that the team medical staff was comfortable bringing players back in groups. The team had a few morning or afternoon lifts. The players gradually reacclimated to the schedule, but some were hesitant to attend meetings and lifts out of concern for their health. After a negative round of testing, Coach Kelly held a team meeting with all the players not in quarantine on the field of the Irish Athletics Complex. Chairs sprawled across the field, each at least 10 feet away from the next. When the meeting concluded, a few players voiced their opinions on the current circumstances. Those who spoke were concerned by the inaccuracy of testing and the ambiguity of the season's future. Kelly did his best to instill confidence that the season would continue. He also made the workouts following his speech completely optional. The chaos of the days prior had made disseminating accurate information difficult, creating significant uncertainty for many members of the program. The teammates, rightfully, requested more transparency in their coach-to-player relationships.

REED: Although I did not agree with everything the players said, I stood behind them on this point. I remember walking into my kitchen, and my roommate, who is not on the team, said to me, "Why aren't you guys practicing today?" to which I responded, "What are you talking about?" Multiple Notre Dame reporters had tweeted about our practice being canceled before any player was directly notified by a coach. This was not the first time something like this had happened. Whether it was the Wake Forest game being canceled or finding out my own teammate has COVID, I didn't particularly appreciate seeing the news on social media before hearing it from a coach.

The schedule showed the players working out after the meeting, but some were uneasy about working out in groups without multiple negative tests. The defense was supposed to run on the outdoor fields while the offense lifted in the gym. Most of the offense ran into the Gug to lift without a problem. On the other hand, the defense was split and some decided to leave.

> **REED:** We huddled together as a unit, ironically, and discussed whether or not it was safe to train. Some already had antibodies and were completely comfortable working out. Others were very aware of the precautions the team had put in place to keep everyone safe and felt protected. And a few players didn't feel entirely safe and decided to leave. At the time, there was so much uncertainty around the short-term and long-term effects of COVID that nobody would force anyone to do anything they were not comfortable doing.

In the Guglielmino Athletics Complex, the strength and conditioning coaches, led by Coach Balis, took every step to ensure player safety while still being able to train vigorously. Each player was required to wear an Under Armour training mask for the entire workout. At the start of every lift, the units were split into four groups, with one strength coach to guide each group from station to station. Each station consisted of 15–20 minutes of different exercises. The equipment at each station was significantly spaced out. The "social distance" between players while they exercised ruled out any possibility of contact tracing within the Gug. At the foot of every piece of equipment were small hand towels and a sanitizing spray bottle. When the players switched stations, they were required to spray and wipe down the equipment thoroughly. Whether it was a bench press, dumbbells, or a pull-up bar, everything was cleaned. The outdoor workouts were relatively easier to make safe. In the stretching lines, players were already separated by at least six feet. All runs took place on the indoor field with all doors open or on one of the adjacent outdoor fields. Due to the fresh air and surplus of field space, players were permitted to take their masks off for the duration of the workout.

A typical week would have coaches running from meeting to meeting, prepping for the next practice. Whether it was watching film on the week's opponent or drawing up plays for the offense to try or for the defense to defend, the coaches were usually in neverending preparation. This week, however, the Gug was quiet. There was no impending matchup for over two weeks. The players had a few days off, but eventually, Coach Kelly wanted the team back in action. The coaches were forced to get creative.

In Coach Lea's first meeting back, he brought the entire defense, or at least what was left of it, into the auditorium. For this meeting, the defense sat especially distanced from one another. Lea talked about the strangeness of this season and the ambiguity that would follow. This meeting was not about scheme or game plan; it was about our team. He put a 30-minute episode from the Netflix documentary series called *The Playbook: A Coach's Rules for Life* up on the big screen. This particular episode highlighted Doc Rivers and his 2008 NBA championship–winning Celtics team. The team had three superstars—Paul Pierce, Ray Allen, and Kevin Garnett—and Rivers described how all three of them were leaders in their own way and that, for the team to be successful, he would have to find a way for them to work together. Someone recommended the word *ubuntu*. Rivers researched the word and described it as "perfect." *Ubuntu* comes from an African Zulu phrase meaning, "A person can only be a person through others." This concept allowed the players to push aside all personal intentions and worry solely about the goals of the team. Rivers described the meaning of *ubuntu* as, "I can't be all I can be, unless you are all you can be. I can never be threatened by you because you're good, because the better you are, the better I am."

> **REED:** This meeting, although like nothing we had ever done before, was oddly engaging. No one's eyes wandered; everyone watched intently and took notes. I felt the episode related greatly to our situation. Our team had an abundance of exceptional athletes, all trying to prove their worth and make it to the League. The documentary certainly struck a chord with the players. Lea always tried to end meetings with big-picture lessons, but hearing from an NBA championship–winning coach was a nice change of pace. In the practices that followed, Jeremiah Owusu-Koramoah would break down huddles with, "Ubuntu on two." It's impossible to tell how much the lessons from the documentary truly resonated with the players, but from my point of view, it seemed to make an impact. In a way, the canceled game and redesigned schedule might have been a small blessing in disguise.

While some players were adapting to the new schedule, others were stuck in quarantine. COVID-positive players were forced to self-isolate, either in their own university-approved off-campus location or in a university-sponsored room, the Morris Inn or some other off-campus apartment.

JOHN: Toward the end of the team's outbreak, I fell victim to COVID as well. Though I'd been quarantined before due to contact tracing, my own positive test forced me into isolation—which I was lucky to be able to do at a friend's vacant condominium, rather than in a hotel room. Luckily, I never really had symptoms, but the medical staff did an outstanding job of monitoring those of us who were forced to be away.

By then, most of us had become pretty accustomed to going to class online, but the reality of exams, group presentations, and the like as the semester continued nevertheless made it a challenge to be stuck at home. Since I caught the tail end of the outbreak, the team began to return to in-person meetings and practices before I could personally come back. I could hear the whistles at practice from where I was staying, which made it that much tougher to stay away—particularly since I didn't feel the least bit sick. Upon my release, I had to undergo a battery of physical tests—on my heart and lungs, primarily—before I could practice. It was a hassle, but it was reassuring to know that, despite all the uncertainty, we'd be taken care of health-wise.

While the Fighting Irish football team was adjusting in its own way, the university had made incredible strides to ensure all students' safety. Many classes had become 100 percent online. Other classes were half online and half in-person, while some other classes were completely in-person. This was particularly rare when compared to schools across the United States. Many universities did not allow students back on campus at all.

Classrooms looked very different from previous years. Some rooms were too small to host any class meetings. Only rooms that were large enough to account for adequate social distancing could be used for in-person lectures. The rooms were flooded with informative posters and floor spots designating approved seating assignments, all plastered with a word that would mark all university pandemic adjustments: HERE. For example, HERE we keep our masks above our nose, HERE we keep social distance, or HERE we sit in the same seat. On the first day of class, students had to log their seat location into the here.nd.edu website. By logging the student's seat, the university would be able to contact trace people who sat adjacent to someone who tested positive.

The website had many other purposes. It was an outlet for students to find information on COVID protocol, find places to eat, gather, work, and lastly, its most commonly visited tab, the COVID report dashboard. Updated daily, the dashboard recorded every test administered, every positive test, and a seven-day trendline. Students often visited the site to see how the university's new adjustment had affected the number of positive tests.

> **JOHN:** It was certainly an adjustment; classes normally held in a conventionally sized classroom were now set up in large auditoriums to allow for social distancing. Teachers taught from behind glass screens and were prevented from speaking with students individually—creating a more sterile (no pun intended) environment than we were used to. Honestly, though, most of us were just happy to be there in person.

Student life on campus was especially different from past years. Dining halls were vacated, and outdoor tents were put up for students to eat their meals safely. No food was allowed in any indoor public areas. Although there were many glum modifications to the campus, a few pleasantries arose in their place. Library Quad was filled with chairs, couches, and fireplaces. In nice weather, students would sit out on the quad and work. From 9:00 to 11:00 PM on Thursdays, Library Quad would host Acousticafe. An event where anyone could sign up to perform on stage, surrounded by string lights and firepits. South Quad was freshly occupied by a large tent of "Quad Lodge" that housed a plethora of socially distant activities, including Ping-Pong, cornhole, and miniature golf.

Some not-so-lucky students would have to put the amenities on hold. Students who tested positive were forced to quarantine, just like the football team, in university-approved spaces. Due to the hectic nature of the first few weeks of school, some were placed in off-campus apartments, while others were put in hotel rooms. Although the locations may have differed, their experiences were relatively similar.

One student who tested positive in August had a typical quarantine. She was feeling symptoms but struggled to get a test through the school. After testing positive at an off-campus site, she uploaded her results to the University Health Services (UHS) online portal. UHS told her a car would come to pick her up, but due to an influx of positive tests in August, the vehicle could not come until the following day. When she was picked up, the car stopped at the stadium to receive her quarantine care package, including information on trash days, mental health resources, and whom to call for different wants and needs. She remained isolated in the on-campus hotel, the Morris Inn, for 10 days. For the first few days, she could choose her food for each meal of the day, but as the days went on and the Morris Inn housed more COVID positives, the meals arrived without preference. UHS did not permit her to leave the room, save for one false fire alarm, where students staggered across the hotel's backyard. Daily calls from the university hotline checked her symptoms and ensured her safety. After a

Zoom call with a St. Liam's doctor from the on-campus hospital, she was cleared to leave. Remarking on her experience in a positive manner, she was thankful for everything the school had done.

> **REED:** Due to the chaos that ensued following the first spike, the university was forced to adapt quickly. Some of my friends documented their experiences through a daily Snapchat story vlog. The adjustments made in response to the spike seemed less than ideal. But then again, the university had to work with what it had during uncertain times.

Another student who tested positive in August had a unique experience. After testing positive at the South Bend Clinic, notifying University Health Services of his roommates for contact-tracing purposes, and pleading to stay in his one-person room with a private bathroom, UHS forced him to drive to an apartment complex on Route 933. Campus dining hall meals were dropped at his door daily. He did not receive any daily calls from the university hotline and argued with UHS over when he would be allowed to leave.

At this point, everyone was confused, and people cluelessly followed orders because that was all the information they had. Students were forced to follow rules they didn't understand for fear of academic repercussions, and the university did its best to keep the students safe with the information it was given. The situation at Notre Dame, although not perfect, was as good as any school in the United States.

Over time, UHS adjusted its protocol to some of the students' requests. Students were now able to quarantine at their off-campus living spaces if they could prove they had their own room and personal bathroom. Students also received extensive testing, including required surveillance testing once a week.

Meanwhile, after a week of intense speculation, news broke on the evening of September 25 that Amy Coney Barrett would, in fact, be nominated to replace Ruth Bader Ginsburg on the United States Supreme Court. It was an exciting moment for many members of the Notre Dame community, but additional COVID-related controversy ensued as evidence surfaced that a number of people at her nomination ceremony had failed to wear masks and maintain proper social distancing. The optics were bad enough as it was, but the number of positive cases among attendees in the weeks that followed was both distracting and embarrassing for a university that had already been in the news for its challenges in combating the virus."

> **JOHN:** It was just the way of the world at that point, but I thought it was really unfortunate to see such a momentous occasion tarnished with a distraction like that.

> **REED:** I commend Notre Dame for the efforts in allowing students to attend in-person classes and maintain a relatively normal college experience. Regardless of the incident, President Jenkins deserves an immense amount of credit for initiating students' return to campus.

All in all, Notre Dame received heavy backlash for being the first to proceed with in-person classes, but the students could not have been more proud of the university. When news spread of the school's positive case levels, rumors floated of a return to all online classes. In response, the student body flaunted its love for the school all over social media with a slight twist on a word the school had chosen to get through the pandemic: We Love It HERE.

OUR BOLD OPINION: Without Notre Dame's return to in-person classes, there is no Notre Dame Football. Without Notre Dame football, there is no college football. ESPN's Gene Wojciechowski put it best in a video posted on September 12 thanking us for joining a conference:

"Without you in the ACC, who knows what would have happened?"

CHAPTER 5

TESTING NEGATIVE

As the college football season pressed on across the country, the Irish slowly worked their way out of the COVID-related purgatory they found themselves in. October 3 had always been scheduled as a bye week, but despite the fact that the Demon Deacons shared the same off week, the canceled matchup from the week prior was rescheduled for the end of the season. Practically speaking, this gave Notre Dame time to get healthy—but also forced the team to deal with a three-week layoff between games, which is virtually unheard of during a regular season in college football. As the affected players began to complete their respective periods of quarantine and isolation, coaches and medical staff members worked on establishing a path forward—which would entail more stringent precautions than the team had put in place prior to the outbreak.

The first and perhaps most significant of these was the use of the stadium locker room during the week. The team's locker room at the Gug wasn't large enough to accommodate the entire roster and maintain social distancing, so approximately 50 players—primarily freshmen and walk-ons—were asked to dress at the stadium before practices. It wasn't an ideal scenario for anyone; it created extra work for the players and staff alike, but it was a necessary precaution given the circumstances. In addition, pregame protocols would look different. The most recent outbreak had been traced to a pregame meal at the DoubleTree hotel in downtown South Bend, demonstrating the inadequacy of those facilities for hosting meetings and meals prior to games. With that, the program decided to use the Century Center—directly across the street—for pregame preparations moving forward. The convention halls and auditoriums would allow the team to minimize contact, hopefully reducing the likelihood of another setback like the one it had just experienced.

> **JOHN:** Admittedly, it took a while to get used to commuting between the stadium and the Gug every day—particularly since this change happened so abruptly. Everything we do is based out of the Gug, from rehab to team meals, so to be detached like that was an adjustment. I understood the reasoning but was disappointed that things had to be that way.

> **REED:** We worked with what we had, and although it was less convenient, we learned to like our new setup. The senior walk-ons were dispersed around the locker room in the Gug, but in the stadium, everyone was a few lockers away. Our proximity made occasions where we had to kill some time much more fun.

And though COVID had proven to be a formidable foe over the previous few weeks, the arrival of game week meant that the team's immediate attention was turned to a more conventional opponent—the Florida State Seminoles. The rivalry between the two teams, though less venerable than some of Notre Dame's others, was nevertheless intense. Forged in the mid-1990s with a trio of closely contested, hard-fought battles between squads led by two legendary coaches Lou Holtz and Bobby Bowden, it had become a premier matchup in college football. Florida State entered the contest at 1–2, having struggled to defeat FCS program Jacksonville State the week prior, but the team's obvious talent—as well as the turmoil that ND had experienced recently—ensured that Saturday's game would be as compelling as those that had come before it.

In a team meeting that Monday, Kelly quickly put to rest any doubts about the ability of FSU's players, referencing the NFL potential of defensive lineman Marvin Wilson, as well as a number of other players on the Seminoles roster. Though they'd gotten off to a slow start, first-year head coach Mike Norvell was well-respected in the sport—and clearly had his team moving in the right direction, despite the challenges that this season had brought. After such a long layoff, it would be a crucially important week of preparation for the Fighting Irish.

After such a long layoff, the staff knew it was important for the team to work its way back into playing shape—"shake the rust off," so to speak. Not only had the entire team been off the practice field for an extended period of time, but many of the players had been ill. Once they had been cleared by the medical staff, they needed to ensure that they had the physical endurance to play four quarters of football. Furthermore, the disruptions that the team had experienced, both at the beginning of the season and more recently, had simply afforded it fewer reps than it had had in previous campaigns. All this meant that this week of practice would be more physical and demanding than a normal week of preparation.

JOHN: I didn't finish up my isolation period until Wednesday of that week, and even then I couldn't fully participate in practice until the results of my tests were in. I was eager to get back, though, so I went in to help signal and do what I could. I was impressed by how long and intense practices were. The offense looked strong, and we were further along than I thought we would be after such a long layoff.

Following Friday's walk-through, the team headed downtown to the DoubleTree and got its first taste of the new pregame protocols. Meals and meetings were held in the Century Center, a large convention hall across the street. Dinner took place in a great hall, a space large enough to hold a small concert. Two players shared each table with a plexiglass divider in the middle, each spaced at least 10 yards from the next. The Friday night special teams meeting was in a theater-style, semicircular auditorium, while the offense and defense unit meetings were in separate ballrooms, where each player sat at his own personal table to take notes. Back in the hotel, each player had his own room and was prohibited from visiting others. On top of that, masks were required at all times.

As kickoff drew closer, 10,409 eager fans gathered in Notre Dame Stadium to see their team play for the first time in three weeks. Despite the chaos and uncertainty of the previous few weeks, it seemed that some sense of normalcy had returned once more in South Bend. Though it was an evening kickoff, the weather was perfect—64 degrees, with no precipitation and a light breeze from the north. The Seminoles won the opening coin toss and deferred, meaning that the fifth-ranked Irish would start with the ball. Tyree returned the opening kick to the 29-yard line, and the Notre Dame offense started the game, hoping to pick up where it had left off against South Florida.

After a first-down completion to senior tight end Brock Wright, however, disaster befell the Irish. As he carried the ball around the left end, Williams was stripped—and Florida State recovered. Just two plays into its return effort, Notre Dame found itself in a tough spot. Though the Seminoles started their drive on the Irish 32, the defense held firm, preventing an FSU first down and forcing a 42-yard field-goal attempt. The kick was good, and the Irish found themselves trailing with just over 12 minutes to play in the first quarter.

> **JOHN:** That was a big moment for us defensively. Allowing them to capitalize on our mistake by scoring a touchdown there would have been disastrous, so even though they were able to score three, it was a victory for us.

> **REED:** Coach Lea's "RBI defense" came into play here. The defense was put on a short field, an obvious disadvantage. RBI defense was a strategy we used to record a score between the opposing team's offense and our defense. If the opposing team scored a touchdown, it was given seven points and the defense zero; if the team made it to the red zone and were held to a field goal, the defense would receive four points and the offense three. Every Monday, we would review the actual score and the RBI score to analyze our performance. Holding FSU to a field goal on this drive was a win for the defense.

The Seminoles lead didn't last very long, as Williams atoned for his previous error by busting loose for a 65-yard gain on the first play of the next drive. Two plays later, Mayer caught a pass from Book for his first career touchdown reception, and the Irish were back in business. A Doerer extra point provided the exclamation point, and Notre Dame took a four-point lead. The Irish defense held strong and forced a punt on the following drive—despite a 31-yard completion that moved FSU across mid-field—giving the offense a chance to extend the lead and take full control of the game.

> **REED:** Once again, the defense was put in a difficult position. The resilience ingrained in each player kept FSU out of the end zone, and this time out of the uprights. Ade sacked the QB for a loss of six and fired everyone up. I could see our team's spirit and energy rise after Ade flexed on the Seminoles.

Starting at their own 24, Book and the rest of the Notre Dame offense wasted no time. Two completions to junior Braden Lenzy brought the Irish across midfield, at which point Williams once again found a hole in the Seminoles defense—running untouched into the end zone for a 46-yard touchdown. After his inauspicious start, he'd become a catalyst for the Irish, tallying over 100 yards on the ground with six minutes left to play in the first quarter. Doerer's extra point was once again perfect, and the home team's lead was extended to 11.

> **JOHN:** In the locker room before the game, Coach Kelly had implored us to start fast and set the tone early in the game. We knew this was a team that could be dangerous if we allowed it to stay in the game, so asserting our dominance early was of paramount importance if we hoped to ultimately come out with the win. Obviously, the early turnover wasn't ideal, but we'd recovered extremely well and established ourselves despite that.

Following another Seminoles three-and-out on the ensuing drive, the Irish appeared to be in the driver's seat. However, Lawrence Keys III was unable to haul in the punt, and FSU recovered. It was the second Irish turnover of the first quarter, and it put the Seminoles inside the Notre Dame 20 to start their drive. They capitalized on the opportunity, relying on carries by quarterback Jordan Travis to score in three plays, narrowing their deficit to four. An Irish three-and-out on the following drive gave Florida State the ball back on its own 29. On third down, three plays after a 17-yard gain on the first play of the drive, Travis found Tamorrion Terry on a go route for a 48-yard touchdown. After having taken a two-score lead, the Irish suddenly found themselves trailing with 38 seconds to play in the first quarter.

> **JOHN:** We brought pressure, hoping to get to Travis before he could make a throw to move the chains on third down. They identified single coverage, and Terry ran an excellent route—gaining separation after a double move. We knew this offense would be explosive, but that play was certainly a wake-up call for our entire unit. It had been a chaotic first quarter, but we knew then that we were in for a dogfight.

Fortunately for the Irish, the offense was able to respond. A 36-yard completion to McKinley closed the quarter in style, and Williams found paydirt six plays later to put the Irish on top once again. Leading 21–17, we forced a three-and-out but couldn't get anything going offensively, punting to the Seminoles with 9:20 to play in the second quarter. Another three-and-out by the FSU offense gave the Irish offense another chance, however, and it took full advantage. It continued its attack on the Seminoles' run defense, though this time it was Tyree—who collected gains of six and 13 on the ground before scampering up the middle for a 45-yard touchdown. Following the extra point, the score sat at

28–17, and it appeared that the Irish had once more established control leading into halftime.

To its credit, however, Florida State refused to go away. A 13-play, 67-yard drive ended in a field goal, which cut its deficit to eight and left the Irish with just 1:17 to work with before halftime. The Seminoles would be receiving the kickoff to start the second half, so they were very much in the game if they could keep it a one-score difference before halftime. Fortunately for Notre Dame, however, Book was able to use his feet to capitalize on a 36-yard Jafar Armstrong kick return, converting three first downs before finding Lenzy for a six-yard score with just 11 seconds to play in the half. Now behind by 15, the 'Noles took a knee to send the game to halftime. After a topsy-turvy half of football, the Irish led 35–20.

> **JOHN:** It wasn't perfect, but after such a long layoff, it was probably unrealistic to expect it to be. Obviously, the turnovers were less than ideal, but we'd shown a lot of promise on both sides of the ball. All things considered, we were in a pretty good spot—the objective moving forward was to build on that momentum and close the game out early in the second half, since we knew they were likely to come out firing.

However, the Seminoles kept clawing their way back. They opened the drive with a 30-yard completion from Travis to Terry, and six plays later scored a touchdown. Down nine, they elected to attempt a two-point conversion to cut their deficit to a touchdown. From the 3, Travis looked to pass but faced interior pressure from junior Jayson Ademilola. He released toward the back of the end zone, but his pass was broken up by D.J. Brown and Shaun Crawford—preserving Notre Dame's two-score lead.

REED: Defensively, Lea was not satisfied with the performance at halftime. We had the speed and the physicality; we just needed to follow through on assignments. Apparently, it took one more drive for the message to sink in. From here on out, the defense would play with a newfound passion and focus, coined by Coach Lea as "targeted aggression."

On the ensuing drive, the Irish overcame a personal foul penalty on the kickoff return and worked their way to their own 37, where Book once again found McKinley for a long completion—this time for 38 yards. After a first-down completion to Davis and a pass-interference penalty against FSU, Book carried around the left side for a three-yard touchdown. A Doerer extra point pushed the margin to 16—where it would stay for the duration of the game. The rest of the contest was a barely reportable battery of punts and turnovers, though there was some intrigue on the Irish sideline as the second half pressed on.

JOHN: Before each drive, it was our responsibility as signalers to make sure that the unit on the field knew which one of us was "live," since some of us were always giving false signals in an effort to prevent sign stealing. And though we had hand signals that we could use to communicate this information, the majority of drives began with a TV timeout—allowing us to audibly tell each position group which of us to pay attention to. However, we discerned during the second half that the FSU-affiliated ball boys on our sideline (essentially, more nondescript versions of "Red Lightning" from a few years ago) had not only been listening in, but had found a way to communicate this information to their own sideline. Obviously, this presented a number of issues, so we made sure the coaching staff knew and were far more subdued in how we communicated with the guys on the field in the future.

Following their 42–26 victory, the Irish returned to their locker room to celebrate. It was their 21st consecutive win at Notre Dame Stadium, and they'd stayed perfect—moving to 3–0. Obviously, it had been a pretty sloppy victory, and there were no illusions about how many corrections would need to be made in the weeks to come. But the fact remained that a win was a win, and it was acknowledged that the team had been lucky to be able to play at all. The game ball was given to team doctor Matt Leiszler, head trainer Rob Hunt, and the rest of the training staff for their hard work and dedication in getting the team healthy enough to play. Before the team sang the fight song, Kelly implored the players to stay vigilant and healthy—reminding them that there was no more flexibility in the schedule to cancel or move games. The Louisville Cardinals would be visiting next week, and he knew that his team needed to be at full strength in order to come out victorious once again.

Following a day off on Sunday, the 3–0 Irish began preparing for the Cardinals—who were led by second-year head coach Scott Satterfield. Notre Dame had opened the season in Louisville the year before, and had been pushed harder than many had anticipated before pulling away to earn a 35–17 victory. So, despite the Cardinals' 1–3 record, there would be no looking past them that week in South Bend. Florida's loss to Texas A&M had caused it to fall in the rankings, allowing the Irish to move up to No. 4 in that week's AP poll. Ahead of the Irish were both Alabama and Georgia, who were also scheduled to meet that Saturday—leaving an obvious path for further advancement if they could take care of business against the Cardinals.

In team meetings on Monday, however, little attention was paid to the national landscape. Though they'd escaped with a win the previous Saturday, players and coaches alike agreed that there was significant room for improvement. With that in mind, Kelly informed his team that it would be a grueling week of practice—in many ways similar to the one before it. When compared to prior teams, he said, this year's group was behind from a reps perspective. Though this was inevitable due to the effects of the pandemic, he believed that the team needed to catch up—and said that this week of practice would be its best opportunity to do so.

JOHN: At that point, I'd been fully cleared to return following my isolation period. I got thrown right back into practice as soon as I was ready, and would be lying if I said it wasn't a demanding, tough few days. It was certainly more physical than it normally would have been at that point in the season, but I completely understood why things had to be that way.

As those arduous few days drew to a close, the team embarked on its traditional Friday preparation routine—meetings at the Gug, walk-through at the IAC, then meals and additional meetings at the Century Center in Downtown South Bend. However, that afternoon, there was some chaos within the signaling squad. Reed's roommate had woken up with a headache and a sore throat, and out of an abundance of caution, the university forced him and his roommates to quarantine until their ill roommate's test results came back. Obviously, this prevented him from traveling with the team to the hotel that night, so John was forced to take his place.

REED: This was one of the most confusing and stressful days of the semester, but everything worked out just fine in the end.

That morning my roommate had told the rest of the house that he wasn't feeling right. He got tested at the university, received a NEGATIVE rapid test, and was waiting on his PCR test results. Later that day, I got a call from University Health Services informing me I had to quarantine until my roommate's test had come back because he was "presumed positive." I responded, saying that wasn't true; he had a negative rapid test. After arguing with the woman, who I know had no control over the situation, I called Coach Lea and informed him of the problem. I told him I might be able to signal in the game tomorrow if my roommate's results come back in time, but I would not be able to make it to the hotel for the night's meetings. Fortunately, our team doctor, Dr. Leiszler, was able to expedite my roommate's test results Saturday morning, and I was able to dress for the game. Yet another stressful inconvenience caused by the coronavirus. In the end, everything worked out, and I was gifted the night off to spend time with my visiting family, a risk they were willing to bear.

JOHN: It had to have been at around 2:00 PM that afternoon—Reed called me, saying that he wasn't allowed to attend practice due to contact tracing and that I would thus need to travel with the team to the hotel. With just 30 minutes or so until meetings began, I called Coach Lea—who confirmed everything he'd said. I'd made the trip to the hotel before, so it wasn't a huge deal, but I did have to leave campus and go back to my house to pack since I hadn't even brought a bag with me to the facility that day. In my estimation, the entire ordeal spoke to how fragile the entire situation, both at Notre Dame and across the country, truly was.

The morning of the game, the team ate breakfast, walked through one more time, then headed north to Notre Dame Stadium. The team met at midfield for a prayer and Coach Lea's final thoughts, then returned to the locker room to get dressed. As players took the field for warmups, virtually everyone began to notice some unusually persistent disrespect from the Louisville players. They were extremely vocal, and some of them went so far as to disrupt Notre Dame's pregame drills. It was certainly unusual, and didn't go unremarked in the Irish locker room immediately before the game.

JOHN: My position coach, Coach Joseph, seemed particularly upset by Louisville's antics. He keeps things on a pretty even keel most of the time, and I'd never seen him so animated as when he challenged us to answer their trash talk with a dominant performance that afternoon. Guys were pretty into it, and it was an intense atmosphere as we listened to Coach Kelly's final thoughts and prayed before returning to the field. I guess they thought they were going to try and intimidate us, but I didn't get the sense that they'd been super successful.

It was an afternoon kickoff, but the weather was windy, cloudy, and markedly cooler than it had been the week before. Daelin Hayes represented Notre Dame at the opening coin toss, which we won. The Irish elected to receive, and things began soon thereafter. Following a touchback on the opening kickoff, they overcame a penalty and a couple negative plays to trudge down the field on a 12-play, 61-yard drive that culminated in a Doerer field goal. After the defense forced a punt, Book and the Notre Dame offense did something similar—though this trip took 15 plays and covered 76 yards, it nevertheless ended in another field goal. With a few seconds left to play in the first quarter, the Irish had controlled the tempo and fought their way to a 6–0 lead.

JOHN: Obviously, we wanted to finish drives, but we had a lot to feel good about early on. We'd been productive and resilient on the offensive side and had completely stifled them defensively. With that being said, things had certainly developed differently than many of us had anticipated. Their first few games had turned into shootouts, so we knew they could score—and score quickly.

REED: The defense was performing excellently on all levels. The defensive line was impassable, the linebackers plumb, and the secondary unyielding. Like clockwork, everyone performed the game plan, each refilling the gaps left by the other—a stark contrast to last Saturday's first half.

After forcing another Cardinals punt, the two teams traded three-and-outs, giving the Irish the ball on their own 4 approximately halfway through the second quarter. From there, Book paced the ND attack with his feet, as well as with first-down completions to Mayer and Tyree, taking six minutes off the clock and establishing a first-and-10 at the Cardinals 14 with just under two minutes to play in the half. Unfortunately, a first-down sack derailed our progress and forced the field-goal team onto the field. Rather than attempt the 31-yard field goal to go ahead by two scores, however, the Irish ran a fake. Bramblett carried the ball toward the left side and gained seven yards, but fell short of the first-down marker—giving Louisville the ball back with the score still 6–0. With under a minute to play in the half, the Cardinals offense was able to advance far enough to attempt a 52-yard field goal as time expired. The kick fell short of the uprights, though, preserving the Irish shutout and maintaining a tenuous six-point lead into halftime.

> **JOHN:** It would have been nice to be ahead two scores as we headed into halftime, but I respect Coach Kelly's decision and admire his aggressiveness in that situation. The defense was playing so well that, in my estimation, it made a lot of sense to go for the jugular there.

At halftime, the defensive coaching staff praised the players for their performance in the first half while imploring them to maintain their momentum through the rest of the game. The Cardinals were slated to receive the opening kickoff, tasking the defense with preserving the slim lead as the second half began.

> **REED:** Kelly applauded the defense while the offense received an encouraging nudge. Lea approached the linebackers with a smile but still bore a plethora of notes and adjustments. It was inspiring to see how hard the players and coaches worked, even when we were playing well.

After allowing two first downs to open the half, the Irish defense appeared to once again have stymied the Louisville attack. On third-and-14 from the Louisville 37, however, quarterback Malik Cunningham scrambled for 11 yards, setting up a manageable fourth down from around midfield. Sensing an opportunity, Satterfield elected to keep his offense on the field. Sticking with what had worked, the Cardinals called a designed quarterback run. Carrying off the right tackle, Cunningham gained another 8 yards, gaining enough for a first down and extending the Louisville drive. Four plays later, following a 29-yard completion from Cunningham to Javian Hawkins, they found paydirt and knotted the score at 6–6. An extra point pushed them ahead, and the onus was suddenly on the Irish offense to reassert control.

> **JOHN:** Letting them off the hook on that third-and-long was disappointing on our part, because we almost certainly could have forced a punt if we'd been able to keep him from escaping the pocket. Going in, we knew Cunningham could make plays with his feet, and we lost contain on that play—which you can't do against a guy with that kind of speed.

On the ensuing kickoff, disaster nearly struck the Irish. Louisville executed a surprise onside kick and recovered, seemingly giving them possession at around midfield. After an officials' review, however, it was determined that a member of the Louisville coverage team blocked an Irish player prior to the ball going 10 yards—forcing a re-kick. This time, the Cardinals kicked off conventionally, and Tyree returned to the Notre Dame 34. Facing a deficit for the first time that afternoon, the Irish offense took the field. After a 14-yard Williams carry to start the drive, it found itself facing a third-and-1 from the Cardinals 45. Still well beyond field-goal range, a conversion was absolutely critical. A jet sweep to McKinley was more than enough, giving Notre Dame a first down at the Cardinals 30. Four plays later, on third-and-8, Book scrambled from 13 yards out for the first Irish touchdown of the afternoon—putting them ahead 12–7. The two-point conversion that would have put them up a touchdown, however, was unsuccessful, keeping the margin at five.

Following this relative outburst of scoring, however, there was a reversion to the mean. On each of the three drives that followed Book's touchdown, neither team made it past midfield, keeping the score at 12–7 into the fourth quarter. With just under eight minutes to play in the fourth, Louisville punted to Notre Dame, which would be forced to begin its drive at its own 23. From there, a combination of savvy clock management and a trio of clutch third-down conversions by McKinley, Skowronek, and Williams allowed the Irish to bleed the clock and escape with a victory. Book's touchdown proved to be the deciding factor, and the Irish escaped with an unremarkable 12–7 win—moving their consecutive home win streak to 22 games.

REED: From 68 total points the week before to a 19-point total this week, I learned never to think I had an accurate prediction of a game's outcome. We had to respect every team we faced, regardless of the message surrounding them. Regardless, the game was an impressive defensive display, not only for the team's stars, but for many players whose work seldom goes unnoticed. We had 10 different players with two or more tackles and seven different players with a tackle for loss.

JOHN: It wasn't a victory anyone felt particularly great about, but a win is a win. Also the defense was a play or two away from pitching a shutout, which marked an obvious improvement from the week before. Beyond that, though, there was just a prevailing sense of fatigue that I could tell the majority of my teammates were feeling. After a tough week of practice, it made sense that guys didn't feel as fresh as they normally would, but I think everything else going on in the world was wearing people down in a way that they hadn't experienced before.

In the locker room after the game, Kelly congratulated the team on a gritty, hard-fought victory and awarded sixth-year senior Shaun Crawford—who led the team in tackles that afternoon—the game ball. As always, he emphasized the importance of safety and vigilance as he released his players for the night, reminding them of the challenges that lay ahead. Barring anything unforeseen, they'd make their long-awaited road debut in Pittsburgh the following week against a rival that always seemed to give Notre Dame a run for its money. Discipline and consistency would be of the utmost importance, and the players knew that their margin for error was slim.

CHAPTER 6

ON THE ROAD AGAIN

Following the brutal slog against the Cardinals the week prior, it didn't take a psychologist to see that the Irish were in dire need of some inspiration. Sure, they were 4–0 and had moved up a spot in the polls to No. 3, but the performances the last two weeks had been inconsistent and fallen short of the standard that players and coaches alike had set for themselves. It had been a tumultuous, taxing season to that point, without a doubt, so some inconsistency was to be expected. Still, the need to improve was obvious. Following a three-week, virus-related hiatus, they had survived—but couldn't count on that to continue to be the case moving forward. Awaiting them this week was the University of Pittsburgh—which had come within a few plays of ruining Notre Dame's undefeated season just two years prior and always seemed to play the Irish close. The Panthers were 3–3, but two of those losses had come by just one point—and they'd been ranked just a couple weeks earlier. Additionally, this would be Notre Dame's first road test of the year—which, with COVID-19 protocols in place, would present its own set of challenges.

During the team meeting on Monday, Coach Kelly acknowledged the team's collective fatigue—which was corroborated by the GPS data collected by the strength staff both on the field and in the weight room. Across the board, the numbers showed less acceleration and explosiveness, as well as substantial fatigue. Simply put, guys were worn down. In his attempt to rectify this issue, Kelly announced plans to reduce the length of practice during the week. No longer would the team spend a full two hours on the practice field on Tuesday and Wednesday, as they had up to that point. The focus would be on precision and intentionality rather than endurance and repetition, hopefully saving the team's legs and allowing them to perform optimally on Saturday.

> **JOHN:** As the season goes on, practices normally get a little lighter, but this was a more dramatic change than what I was used to. Having so much data available makes decisions like that quite a bit easier to substantiate, but the staff deserves a lot of credit for following the science to put the team in the best position possible down the stretch.

> **REED:** It's impressive to see, firsthand, how much technology plays into football. We use GPS tracking data to test top speeds and output. We use full body heating and cooling pads for recovery. In the past, when we knew we were playing at a loud stadium, we listened to high volume crowd noise through massive speakers on the practice field to prepare. The coaches and signalers use noise-canceling headsets to communicate. Even on the sideline during games, we have portable electronic massage guns for muscle cramps. Coaches must use every technological innovation they can to help their players if they want to win in the modern era.

Until Saturday, it was unclear whether Pitt's star quarterback Kenny Pickett would be able to play as he nursed an ankle injury—forcing the Notre Dame defense to game-plan for two quarterbacks. This presented a challenge for a defense hoping to maintain its momentum from a strong week prior. However, with less wear and tear on their bodies, the Irish embarked on a productive week of practice.

Under normal circumstances, the team would fly out Friday morning for an away game—often leaving campus immediately following the walk-through. COVID protocols, however, sought to minimize travel-related exposure—resulting in significant changes to Notre Dame's pregame travel arrangements. Rather than fly to the site of the away game for dinner and meetings, everything was held in the Century Center in Downtown South Bend. N95 masks were required on team buses and planes, and passengers were intentionally spaced out so as to comply with social-distancing guidelines. Upon arrival, players were expected to grab a snack then head immediately to their rooms—each player had his own—and not fraternize in the lobby or in other shared spaces.

The team arrived in Pittsburgh without incident but was unfortunately awoken on Saturday morning by some devastating news from South Bend—early that morning, two Notre Dame students had been killed after being hit by a car just east of campus. As the team prepared to play, many of the details remained hazy, but hearing of such a tragedy cast a pall over the team's pregame preparation. Though the players had been notified via email, Coach Kelly nevertheless informed the entire group at the hotel that morning, urging everyone to keep the families of those involved in their prayers.

JOHN: To be awoken by that news was just awful. I didn't know the victims personally, but I knew several people that did—and seeing their grief firsthand in the days and weeks that followed was truly heartbreaking. Just an unspeakably tragic event.

There was insufficient space at the Pittsburgh Airport Marriott to host a pregame meal, so the team arrived at Heinz Field early. Everyone ate in an enormous hospitality area, then proceeded to the locker room to begin their preparation. It was the first (and only) time that season that the Irish would play on a natural surface, so much of the players' focus during warmups was centered on feeling out the turf. They'd done their best to prepare—practicing on grass in South Bend that week—but every field is different, and Notre Dame's skill players weren't the sort to leave anything to chance.

> **REED:** I was quite impressed with Heinz Field. We dined in a refined hospitality area attached to the main concessions and walkways inside the stadium. Steelers memorabilia covered the walls. At that moment I realized I was even more grateful to play at a stadium that was ours alone. Sharing a stadium with an NFL team would diminish the school's tradition and achievements. Yet another reason Notre Dame football is unmatched.

As the Irish looked across the field, they saw a Pittsburgh team that looked energetic and excited about the day's matchup. Word had surfaced that Pickett wouldn't, in fact, be playing, but that didn't appear to discourage the Panthers. They were wearing alternate uniforms, which wasn't uncommon for teams hosting Notre Dame, but nevertheless signified the importance of this game for their program. Any doubt over whether Notre Dame would be getting Pitt's best shot quickly dissipated as kickoff drew nearer.

> **JOHN:** Pitt has such cool uniforms normally, so I have no idea why they decided to wear those ugly black and gray ones. I can't imagine that the players liked them that much, but who knows?

Following the teams' emergence from their respective locker rooms, each sent a captain to midfield for the coin flip. Notre Dame's representative was Pittsburgh native Robert Hainsey, who won the toss and elected to receive. After a touchback on the opening kickoff, Book and the Irish offense took the field, hoping to improve on their anemic performance from the week before.

The drive began slowly, but a third-down scramble by Book kept the drive alive. He found Mayer on another third down to move the Irish past midfield, then found Avery Davis in the flat for 14 yards following a first-down incompletion. On first-and-10 from the Pitt 29-yard line, a Kyren Williams carry was negated by a face-mask penalty that moved Notre Dame back 15 yards. A 10-yard Book scramble brought up second-and-11. The Irish aligned with four wide receivers, and with time to throw, Book found Northwestern transfer Ben Skowronek on a crossing route over the middle. After leaping to make the grab, Skowronek raced 20 yards into the end zone—scoring a touchdown on his first catch in a Notre Dame uniform. With just over 10 minutes to play in the first quarter, the Irish had drawn first blood.

JOHN: From the moment he arrived in January, Ben earned the respect of his teammates with his work ethic, toughness, and commitment. He'd been dealt a tough hand with injuries early in the year, so it was awesome to see him break through like that early in this game—particularly since we knew we'd need his talent and experience down the stretch.

Following a kick return to the Pittsburgh 36, the Panthers offense—led by backup quarterback Alex Yellen—took the field. Despite struggling with his accuracy, he was able to convert on two consecutive third downs, moving his offense into field-goal range.

However, from the Notre Dame 27, the Irish defense caused three straight incompletions—forcing the Pitt field-goal team onto the field. Kicker Alex Kessman connected from 45 yards, cutting the deficit to four. As they had many times before, the Irish defense had firmed up when it counted—holding the opposing offense to three points.

Notre Dame's progress on the ensuing drive was stymied by a 15-yard personal foul penalty against offensive tackle Liam Eichenberg, and it was forced to punt from its own 27 after briefly crossing midfield. Pittsburgh's next effort offensively went nowhere, and a third-down sack by senior Myron Tagovailoa-Amosa forced a Panthers punt. From there, the two teams traded punts, giving the Irish possession with just under 12 minutes to play in the first half. The defense had preserved the four-point lead with two consecutive stops, but the offense failed to build on it. Determined to change that, Book began the drive with an 18-yard scramble that brought the Irish to their own 31. Following an incompletion and a sack, however, the Irish offense found itself in a forbidding position—third-and-14 from its own 27.

Hoping to get off the field, the Panthers defense brought pressure, forcing Book to release quickly down the left sideline. Eager to build on his early success, Skowronek split two defenders to not only make the catch, but also sprint an additional 35 yards into the end zone. After not recording a catch in any of the first three games, he'd suddenly become a catalyst for the Irish—who now led 13–3. A Doerer extra point stretched the lead to 11, and Notre Dame appeared to have taken the drivers' seat in this contest.

JOHN: That second touchdown removed any residual doubt—this was Benny's coming-out party. He'd been remarkably productive at Northwestern, so even though we knew it was just a matter of time, we were all extremely glad to see him break through the way he did that game. It couldn't have come at a better time for us, either.

After the Panthers returned the kickoff to their own 31, the Irish defense continued their dominant performance—forcing a three-and-out and giving the offense the ball once again. Unable to extend the lead, however, Notre Dame punted the ball right back. An illegal-formation penalty moved Pitt up to its own 40—providing the Panthers with their best starting field position they'd had all day. Following a completion that moved them across midfield, however, Yellen threw over the middle of the field—failing to account for the presence of Erie, Pennsylvania, product Bo Bauer. The native son intercepted the pass, returning it into Panthers territory and giving his offense the opportunity to start on a short field. The offense took full advantage, capping an eight-play, 46-yard drive with a Kyren Williams touchdown that ultimately widened the Irish lead to 18 points.

REED: We quickly figured out Pitt's offensive line could not handle our defensive line. Coaches Lea and Elston went back and forth on strategies to prevent our D-line from easing off. They switched up fronts and sent blitzes and edge rushes constantly. We knew early on this offense could be shut down from the line of scrimmage, forcing the quarterback to make some questionable throws. I was so happy for Bo after his interception. Yes, it went right into his hands, but he is one of the hardest working guys on the team and always knows his assignments. He was in perfect position to cut the pass off, and it was well deserved.

With a minute-and-a-half to play before halftime, the Panthers would likely have one chance to cut into the deficit and salvage some momentum. An 11-yard carry on first down enlivened the Pitt faithful, but two negative plays on the following series left them once more behind the chains. After a loss of two on third-and-13, the Irish used a timeout—stopping the clock and forcing the Panthers punt team onto the field. To most informed observers, their intent was clear: send heavy pressure to hopefully disrupt the punt, giving them one more chance to score before halftime. However, such obvious insights were evidently lost on the Pitt sideline. They completely failed to block defensive end Isaiah Foskey—who stands 6'5" and weighs nearly 260 pounds—as he ran unimpeded into the backfield. He not only blocked the punt, but recovered it in the end zone for an Irish touchdown—extending the lead to 24 with just a few seconds left in the half. A Doerer extra point made it a four-score game, and a dispirited Pitt team simply ran out the clock, seemingly begging for mercy as time expired.

> **JOHN:** It benefited us, so I'm not complaining, but it was inexcusable that they allowed that punt to be blocked. That was the one thing that they absolutely couldn't let happen in that scenario, and they did—giving us a huge boost going into halftime. At that point, we knew—a stop and a score, and this one would be over.

At halftime, Kelly urged the team to build on its strong performance in the first half. This was no time to take our foot off the gas, he said. Our team needed to demonstrate, to the world but also to ourselves, that we could play four quarters of dominant football. The mantra he coined for the second half was to "Play Dangerous!" Armed with motivation for the second half, the Irish returned to the field. Since they had taken the ball to start the game, the defense would be up first.

REED: After holding Pitt to 19 yards and a fourth-and-long deep in their territory, Salerno ran onto the field to receive the punt. The ball flew high in the air as Pitt moved closer and closer to Salerno. We all expected him to wave his arm in the air, signaling a fair catch, but he never did. He caught the ball and was promptly tackled by a throng of Panthers. As Salerno ran off the field, Coach Kelly shouted at him, "Fair catch that!" to which Salerno playfully replied, "You said, 'Play dangerous,' Coach!" and jogged along the other way—a funny moment on the sideline. Coach Kelly smiled and shrugged. Salerno had a good point.

Pittsburgh's punt gave the offense the opportunity to embark on a 14-play, 72-yard drive that culminated in a Doerer field goal that extended their lead to 28. An Owusu-Koramoah interception on the next drive set up a Michael Mayer touchdown, and Notre Dame led 38–3 with just over four minutes left in the third quarter. On the first play of the next Panthers drive, another interception—this time by graduate transfer cornerback Nick McCloud—gave the Irish offense excellent field position. A Pittsburgh personal foul moved us into the red zone, where C'Bo Flemister stampeded across the goal line for another score, making it 45–3.

With the game well in hand, Notre Dame began to play conservatively while substituting liberally—protecting their star players while keeping as much of their playbook as possible hidden from future opponents. On the Pitt sideline, however, head coach Pat Narduzzi not only kept his defensive starters on the field but also sent aggressive, exotic blitzes at Notre Dame's inexperienced second-string offensive line. Predictably, this upset the Notre Dame coaching staff, who had simply hoped to give several younger players some meaningful game experience against a legitimate opponent.

JOHN: Obviously, I found what they were doing to be pretty tacky, but the discussion that occurred over the headset was hilarious. The coaches were pretty irritated by the whole thing, since the outcome had clearly been decided long before. In games like that, there's usually an unspoken understanding that both sides should do what they can to make sure things end as quickly and painlessly as possible, but they clearly weren't on board. In all honesty, we're just lucky nobody got hurt.

The fourth quarter was uneventful—a series of punts before a 14-play, almost eight-minute drive by the Irish brought the game to a close. The final score remained 45–3—a strong performance by a Notre Dame team in dire need of a dominant effort. After the game, Coach Kelly congratulated his players, but reminded them that there were bigger, tougher tests coming. Not only would they travel to Atlanta to face Georgia Tech the following week— the matchup against the No. 1 Clemson Tigers was now just two weeks away. He emphasized the need for consistent improvement, as well as vigilance amid the pandemic, which continued to rage across the United States. In keeping with this theme, the team ate its socially distanced postgame meal in the bleachers at Heinz Field before heading to the airport for the short flight home.

Yet, even though Notre Dame returned to South Bend 5–0, Ohio State—who had thoroughly beaten Nebraska in their almost comically late season opener—jumped ahead of them in the polls, relegating them once more to fourth. After taking Sunday off, the Irish jumped into a normal week of preparation for Georgia Tech—just as political developments relevant to Notre Dame and the entire nation arose from Washington, D.C.

On the evening of Monday, October 26—just eight days before Americans headed to the polls to vote in the 2020 presidential election—Amy Coney Barrett, a Notre Dame alumna and law professor, was narrowly confirmed by the United States Senate to a seat on the Supreme Court. Her confirmation hearings had been surprisingly uncontroversial, but her investiture nevertheless marked an important yet contentious event for the university community. As the first Notre Dame graduate on the nation's highest court, she was a point of pride for many students, faculty, and alumni. However, Father Jenkins' failure to wear a mask at her nomination ceremony weeks before had been an embarrassing moment for an institution that had struggled publicly with its management of the virus, and many students objected to her confirmation on procedural grounds—believing that no nomination should have occurred until after the election. Protests occurred on campus in the days that followed, only adding to the tension and chaos that was the 2020 election season.

> **JOHN:** Politics aside, most of the guys I lived with realized that it was pretty unique to be living just a couple blocks away from a newly confirmed justice on the Supreme Court. We fashioned ourselves as a thoughtful, neighborly group of young men, so we naturally thought that it would be a nice gesture to drop off a gift of some sort. None of us are bakers or craftsmen, however, so the best idea we could think of was a case of beer. Upon further scrutiny, though, we realized that the Secret Service (or whoever was in charge of her security) probably wouldn't let her or her family consume anything left on her doorstep by unidentified well-wishers, so we ultimately scrapped the idea.

At the Gug, however, the team enjoyed another productive week of practice—seemingly insulated from the political tension.

After the prior week's result, it was clear that Coach Kelly's gamble had paid off. Georgia Tech prep was similarly structured, with a focus on quality over quantity as far as reps were concerned. Under second-year head coach Geoff Collins, the Yellow Jackets had ditched the triple-option offense they had been known for in the first couple decades of the 21st century. Nevertheless, they promised to be a handful to prepare for—freshman quarterback Jeff Sims had formidable talent around him and had been steadily improving as the season progressed. There was no doubt that they were better than their 2–5 record, and it was clear that in order to win this game, the Irish defense would need to build on its success from the previous two weeks.

Following the Friday walk-through in South Bend, the team ate and held meetings before departing for Atlanta. Things carried on much as they had the week prior—limited contact at the hotel and an early bed check to ensure that everyone had the chance to get a good night's sleep. The next morning, the defense held another walk-through in the parking garage attached to the hotel before heading downtown to Bobby Dodd Stadium.

JOHN: We have a fair number of guys on our defense from the Greater Atlanta area—Kyle Hamilton, K.J. Wallace, Isaiah Pryor, and J.D. Bertrand—so Coach Lea's message was centered around making sure that we represented well for each of them in their return home. I'm certain it was a big moment for each of them, and I'm glad they knew their brothers were behind them.

REED: Not known for making jokes, Coach Lea attempted to lighten the mood after we finished running around, preparing for different plays on the second floor of a grimy parking garage. He remarked on the garage's shadiness and how he could almost picture a young Bertrand and Hamilton sneaking about in it. As most of his jokes ended, a player or two would laugh or smile, and Lea would thank them. The effort was usually funnier than the joke itself, but we all appreciated Lea for what he was—a great coach and a terrible comedian.

It was warm and sunny in the Peach State that afternoon—a perfect day for football. Warmups went smoothly, and it appeared that among the 11,000 fans in attendance that day, a substantial minority were partial to the Irish. The home team won the opening coin flip and elected to defer, giving Notre Dame the ball to start the game. Tyree caught the ball on the goal line and elected to try his luck, managing a 19-yard return before being tackled— leaving 81 yards between the Irish and paydirt. And though it took 15 plays and nearly nine minutes to get there, a Joe Wilkins Jr. touchdown started the Irish off on the right foot—giving them a 7–0 lead before the Yellow Jackets even had the chance to touch the ball.

> **JOHN:** Coach Kelly often talks about "imposing your will" on an opponent, and I felt like the offense certainly did that on that first drive. They converted four third downs and took complete control of the game's tempo, sending an indelible message to GT from the first snap.

Following the score, the Irish defense maintained control of the game—forcing a punt and giving the offense the ball back with a lead, as well as good starting field position. Book and Georgia native C'Bo Flemister picked up where they left off the drive before, using a Georgia Tech personal foul to push into the red zone for the second time that afternoon. On second-and-8, however, a Kyren Williams fumble was recovered by Yellow Jackets defensive back Zamari Walton, who outraced the Irish offense and returned it 93 yards for a score. Just seconds before, the Irish had appeared primed to take a two-score lead. Now, as the second quarter began, the game was suddenly tied.

> **JOHN:** It was obviously unfortunate that that happened, but it challenged us to adapt quickly and respond to adversity in a way that we hadn't so far that season. We were a little stunned, to be sure, but we ultimately proved to ourselves that we could take a blow like that and still get our feet back underneath us.

> **REED:** I knew no one had taken the touchdown harder than Kyren. After watching him throughout this season, I knew he would make a point to right his wrong later on the field, and I believe Rees was aware of his resiliency as well.

Seven plays later, however, Notre Dame had reasserted their dominance. Williams and Tyree paced the Irish offense as they marched down the field, and a two-yard Williams touchdown again moved them ahead. Doerer's extra point made the score 14–7, placing the onus on the Irish defense to hold the line and allow the offense to extend the lead before halftime. They answered the call, forcing a three-and-out. The Yellow Jackets brought the punt team on once more, and Salerno fair caught at the Notre Dame 24 with 8:58 to play in the second quarter.

Despite a first-down completion to Georgian Tommy Tremble on the drive's opening play, the Irish offense stalled, answering GT's punt with one of their own. On the ensuing drive, the Yellow Jackets worked their way past midfield, managing a first down before facing a fourth-and-2 from the Notre Dame 45. Following a timeout, Collins elected to keep his offense on the field—setting up a critical down for both sides. The ball was snapped, and Sims faked a handoff before pitching back to running back Jahmyr Gibbs. In his homecoming, Hamilton couldn't be fooled, and he knifed into the backfield to stop Gibbs for a six-yard loss. With just under four minutes to play, the Irish once again had the ball in opposing territory.

> **JOHN:** Kyle read it perfectly, and he shot inside of the pulling tackle—who, frankly, had no chance—to make a huge play for us. We'd allowed their crowd to stay in it up to that point, but that stop definitely took some of the wind out of their sails.

Facing a short field, the offense recorded two first downs before settling for a field goal from 32 yards out. Doerer connected, and the Irish took a two-score lead. Despite having nearly two minutes with which to work, Georgia Tech was unable to cut into the deficit, sending the game to halftime with the Irish ahead 17–7. The defense had performed remarkably well in the first half, and the offense had a lot to feel good about. If it hadn't been for that one disaster of a play, Notre Dame very well could have been leading 24–0.

At halftime, Kelly's message was simple—build on the dominance from the first half while limiting mistakes. At that point, it wasn't just about winning this game—it was about using the second half as a springboard into the following week's preparation. That couldn't happen if the defense allowed GT, who was set to receive the second-half kick, to score and make it a one score game, so the directive was clear: get a stop and a score.

REED: I was surprised yet thrilled with Kelly's halftime message. Usually, he never speaks about the scoreboard, but this game, he really wanted us to finish strong. Part of it seemed personal, but also he wanted to use a dominant victory as an on-ramp into next week's preparation, and I was all for it.

Following a touchback on the opening kickoff, however, the Irish defense got off to a rocky start. A personal foul on the first snap was soon followed by an impressive 39-yard Yellow Jackets completion—putting the Irish defense on its heels just seconds into the third quarter.

JOHN: Though they hadn't been able to manage much in the first half, you began to see glimpses of how dangerous their offense could be on that drive. All things considered, we covered that long pass pretty well, but Sims fit it in a tight window for an explosive play.

After a false-start penalty, Georgia Tech looked to throw. Fortunately for Notre Dame, defensive end Daelin Hayes won his matchup against the GT right tackle and burst into the backfield, getting to an unsuspecting Sims before he could make his primary read. Not content with a sack, he jarred the ball loose. Myron Tagovailoa-Amosa recovered, averting a crisis for the Irish defense and returning the ball to the offense on the Notre Dame 35.

REED: The fumble recovery triggered a jolt of energy within the defense. What made this unit so unique was one player's ability to motivate everyone. On offense and defense, every player fed off the success of others—there was never any maliciousness or jealousy. The players genuinely wanted their friends to triumph so that the team could win.

Aware of their good fortune, the Irish offense took full advantage of the turnover. A third-down scramble by Book moved them across midfield—and a 31-yard completion to Javon McKinley on the following play brought them into the red zone. From there, Williams shouldered the load for Notre Dame, slicing his way through the Yellow Jackets defense to increase the Irish lead. With 10:43 to play in the third quarter, the score was 24–7. Though they had taken the scenic route to start the half, Notre Dame had established a three-score lead as the home stretch neared.

After forcing a punt on the following drive, the Irish offense failed to close the door—punting back to the GT offense with just under seven minutes left in the third quarter. A 10-play, 53-yard drive ultimately proved fruitless for the Yellow Jackets, as a 42-yard field goal fell well short and well right of the uprights—keeping the margin at 17. Book, McKinley, and Williams took full advantage, proceeding to embark on a touchdown drive that stretched the Irish lead to 24 and brought the game into the fourth quarter. A Georgia Tech touchdown midway through the quarter proved to be too little, too late—the game ended 31–13, and the Irish moved to 6–0. It had been a workmanlike victory, celebrated less than perhaps any that had come before it that season. The focus among coaches and players alike immediately turned to what was to come the following week.

CHAPTER 7

GAME OF THE CENTURY

As the final seconds of their 31–13 victory over Georgia Tech ticked away at Bobby Dodd Stadium, an unmistakable sense of anticipation fell over the Fighting Irish. Earlier that day, the Trevor Lawrence–less Clemson Tigers had survived a formidable challenge from Boston College, setting up a matchup of undefeateds to be held at Notre Dame Stadium the following Saturday. In the locker room after the game, Coach Kelly was characteristically blunt about both the team's performance and the challenges the team would face moving forward. Though they'd done a lot of good things against the Yellow Jackets that day, the Irish knew they would need to sharpen up substantially prior to the following Saturday's game. No longer would there be such a disparity in talent that minor errors in discipline or execution could simply be glossed over. For the first time this season, Notre Dame would face a team just as—if not more—talented than they were. Not only that, but this was the biggest game to be held on campus in over a decade, and—at least for the week ahead—the center of the college football universe would be in South Bend. ESPN's *College GameDay* would be in town, and kickoff was set for 7:30 PM on NBC—with Mike Tirico and Tony Dungy on the call. The stage was set, and any pretense of this week's matchup being "just another game" fell quickly by the wayside.

REED: Never has a win felt so much like a loss. We knew the challenges the next weekend would hold and understood that that day's performance would not be enough to get the job done. Stern faces replaced the typical post-win cheer. The upcoming game was our shot to prove that we belonged and silence the hate that followed our 2018 Clemson loss. Looking around the room, I knew no one would take this game for granted.

JOHN: Since Pittsburgh week, Coach Kelly's message had been consistent. No longer could we afford to merely focus on the team immediately in front of us—each week we needed to grow and improve to be able to meet the goals we would face later in the season. Admittedly, after such a close victory over Louisville, I was skeptical about this approach. Since the moment I began playing sports, I'd always been taught that the next game was the most important one, and that looking too far ahead was a recipe for disaster. However, as we left the locker room and headed to the airport, his approach made more sense. It was a risky move, no doubt, but it was the only way to get the team prepared for such a big game. Things like that are why he's so good at what he does—and why he's had the success he's had everywhere he's been.

Further complicating matters was the presidential election, to be held on Tuesday, November 3. And though Election Day always marks an inflection point in American society, this year was different—even in the world of college athletics. In response to popular demand, the NCAA mandated that no teams were to hold practice on Election Day so that student-athletes could exercise their civic duty. Practically, this meant that both Clemson and Notre

Dame would need to adjust their preparation schedules during an already chaotic week—no small task given the circumstances and gravity of this particular matchup. In South Bend, this manifested itself in the form of Sunday meetings and workouts—much to the chagrin of coaches, players, and support staff eager for a chance to rest and recover after two consecutive road games.

> **JOHN:** Though I commend the NCAA for their support of civic participation, I felt like this was yet another well-intentioned effort that practically made little sense. Our staff had done a tremendous job of getting the entire team registered to vote, and the vast majority of us had voted by absentee ballot prior to Election Day. We went out of our way to take care of it ahead of time, and yet we still felt like we were at a disadvantage.

For the Irish, Mondays (or Sunday, in this instance) are used for review of the previous game, as well as the scouting report for the following week's game. Corrections are made, congratulations and criticisms are given, and the book is closed on the previous week. By the end of the day, the focus is completely on the following week's opponent. Defensively, the focus was squarely on Clemson's freshman quarterback, D.J. Uiagalelei—who, in his first collegiate start, had completed nearly 75 percent of his passes while throwing for 342 yards and two touchdowns. He may not have been Trevor Lawrence, but the Irish defense quickly realized they would have to deal with him just the same.

> **REED:** I had mixed feelings when I first learned of Lawrence's positive COVID test. I knew it might give us a better chance of winning, but I also wanted to play the best. That being said, adjusting to COVID and limiting the spread was a new aspect

of the season. Players had to be undoubtedly COVID-free to be allowed to strap on the pads. Our team doctors Matt Leiszler and Rob Hunt, did a fantastic job adapting to these unchartered waters and keeping the team safe. There is something to be said for keeping COVID out of our facilities...especially around big games.

JOHN: I actually remember where I was when I first learned of Trevor Lawrence's positive COVID test. I was out to eat at the Lauber in South Bend, and when I saw the news on the TV behind the bar, I couldn't believe my eyes. I think my reaction might have offended the company I was with, but you couldn't help but think about the implications of something like that. Having recently been quarantined myself, I did the math and soon realized he wouldn't be able to play against us. I thought it was a big deal at the time, but after seeing D.J. play against BC, I quickly realized that there wouldn't be much of a drop-off.

Joining Lawrence on the injured/sick list, however, were a number of the Tigers' best players on the defensive side of the ball. Middle linebacker James Skalski—the unquestioned leader of the Clemson defense—had missed the two previous games with a groin injury, while defensive tackle Tyler Davis and linebacker Mike Jones Jr. were also ruled out. Additionally, defensive end Xavier Thomas would be unable to play in the first half due to his ejection for targeting in the prior week's contest. Though Lawrence's absence received the most attention, those in the know at both programs realized the potential impact of these holes in the Tigers defense. Even for a team as deep as Clemson, the loss of three all-conference performers on one side of the ball is extremely challenging to overcome. Though the talent behind these players was certainly worthy of respect, the Notre Dame offense sensed an opportunity.

> **REED:** Outside of teaching the intricate details of his defense, Coach Lea always made a point to incorporate a life lesson into his meetings. This week's lesson had some not-so-subtle implications. Lea told a story he had heard from a friend who coached Aaron Donald, three-time NFL defensive player of the year, at Pitt. After one of Pitt's road losses, the team would fly home late at night. Upon arrival, most of the team quickly dropped their things off at the facilities and went home to sleep. Aaron Donald did not. He would go directly from the bus to the film room, watch the entire game, and write everything he did wrong on the whiteboard. When the coach came in the next morning, the whiteboards would be filled with notes, questions, and comments on his play. What Coach Lea was really saying was that he wanted to see the linebackers in the film room outside of our regular schedule. If there was any week to channel your inner Aaron Donald, it was this week.

> **JOHN:** I was on the scout team that week, and I thought the offensive game plan did a fantastic job of isolating our relative strengths and their relative weaknesses—particularly given the circumstances. Obviously, our offensive line had done a tremendous job to that point, and their losses in the front seven left them shorthanded. I can remember talking it over early in the week with Gus Ragland, the graduate assistant who led the defensive scout team, and being both impressed and excited for what was to come. If we could establish the run game and give Ian the chance to get outside the pocket and extend plays, it wasn't difficult to see things going well for us offensively.

John (25) and Reed (50) in pregame warmups before Florida State

On the field before the game, Coach Lea identifies the defense's three main focus points.

After defeating Louisville, the team sings a socially distanced "Alma Mater."

Ben Skowronek scores a touchdown in the Irish rout of Pittsburgh.

Against Georgia Tech, John (25) meets with the defensive backs during a timeout.

Masked up and socially distant groups of students (left) cheer on the Fighting Irish.

Jeremiah Owusu-Koramoah (facing page) takes the fumble recovery in for a touchdown against the Clemson Tigers..

The defensive signalers get the calls in as the Irish square off against Louisville

Matt Salerno evades Boston College defenders as poster board cutout fans "cheer on" their team from the stands.

Amid fog and flames, the Fighting Irish take the field in Charlotte, North Carolina, for the ACC Championship Game.

Kyle Hamilton rallies with his teammates after intercepting a pass by Clemson's Trevor Lawrence in the ACC Championship Game..

After a stop on defense, Reed cheers on the Irish offense in AT&T Stadium during the College Football Playoff versus the Alabama Crimson Tide.

The Class of 2021's parting gift to Notre Dame Stadium.

Following Monday's practice, the Irish found themselves with some spare time, as Election Day provided them with the aforementioned day off from team activities. For a group so used to maintaining a strict routine, this presented a significant disruption—and for the less politically inclined members of the team, perhaps afforded them some time to tune into the national conversation surrounding Saturday's game. Some in the media, aware of Clemson's injury situation and already looking ahead to an ACC Championship Game a month-and-a-half later, began discussing the idea that Saturday's game wouldn't ultimately matter as the playoff picture ultimately defined itself. On ESPN's *First Take*, college football pundit extraordinaire Paul Finebaum discussed ad nauseam the path the Tigers would need to take, presumably following a loss, to still make the playoff—suggesting that Lawrence's absence would totally change the perception of the game in the eyes of the selection committee. Furthermore, it seemed that he wasn't alone in believing that. Predictably, this didn't sit well in South Bend.

REED: I understand the reasoning behind these conversations, but nothing positive came from them. Neither side benefited from hearing that this game carried less meaning. To me, it seemed like the media was causing an unnecessary disturbance to create drama around what was a phenomenal matchup between two of college football's greatest powerhouses.

JOHN: I can remember turning the TV on to hear a discussion about exactly this. It's frustrating as a player, because something like this was completely beyond our control. As much as you try to block stuff out, I'd be lying if I said this perception wasn't something that certainly got discussed in meetings that week. More motivation, I suppose, but I still think it was disrespectful to both teams to be pushing that narrative before the game was even played.

Following the day off, however, the week continued on surprisingly smoothly. As Grit Wednesday turned to Attention to Detail Thursday, the team grew increasingly comfortable with the plan. Thursday practice was held in Notre Dame Stadium—as is customary before home games—giving the Irish a chance to envision what was to come the following Saturday. Practice was crisp and detailed, and it appeared that the team had gotten through the week more or less healthy. Friday's walk-through was similarly uneventful, which was a good sign given all the chaos that the year had brought so far.

However, in team Mass that Friday afternoon, team chaplain Father Nate Wills gave the team medals that featured *Stella Maris*—Latin for "Star of the Sea." This gift by itself wasn't anything particularly unusual, since the team receives a medal prior to every game, but this was different. Just once a year is Mary, Our Lady—the namesake of the university, of course—depicted on the medal. Not only was this the game where she was featured, but she was presented like the North Star—"shining proudly in the heavens." It seemed almost too perfect, given the circumstances, and it would have been hard to find a man in that locker room who didn't feel particularly inspired that day.

As the sun rose over South Bend on November 7, the energy on campus was undeniable. It was an unseasonably warm, sunny day—one that you'd expect in late September, rather than early November—which promised a pleasant playing and viewing experience but dispelled any hopes of a weather-related home-field advantage for the Irish. As some of the players gathered in the players' lounge prior to that morning's shake-out, they—along with the millions of other Americans tuned into *GameDay* that morning—were informed by Rece Davis, from inside Notre Dame Stadium just a stone's throw away, that former Vice President Joe Biden had been officially declared the winner of Tuesday's presidential election. On a day that was supposed to be all about football, it was a strange juxtaposition—but politics aside, it added a gravitas to the day's events beyond what already existed.

Following the shake-out, the travel squad returned to the hotel. After a short rest, the team gathered in the Century Center's amphitheater room across the street. Quiet and focused, they patiently waited for Coach Kelly to begin his speech. The players sat with their masks up, spread out with three to four seats between them. With the players focusing intently on Kelly, he took the floor and paced confidently as he addressed his team. He began by commenting on the numerous texts he had received leading up to the game—most of which were well-wishes, focused generally around the theme of "good luck." However, he singled out a text from former Notre Dame wide receiver Chris Finke, who texted saying that he would wish the team good luck, but luck is for the unprepared. Coach Kelly focused on the underlying message of Chris's text. He acknowledged that the team was indeed prepared and didn't need luck. All we needed to do was show Clemson our preparation. "Welcome to our preparation!" he shouted. Eager grins overtook the players' intense facades. They were ready, and they knew it. A confident group of Fighting Irish loaded up the buses and headed to the stadium. The time for preparation was over. Performance was all that was left.

REED: Coach Kelly's pregame speech that afternoon was one of the most moving, powerful, and accurate speeches I had heard him give. I have never seen our team practice so hard. In weeks where we faced weaker opponents, I could tell when the guys had taken their foot slightly off the gas. Other weeks, I watched the guys take the opponent extremely seriously and work insanely hard. This week was a whole other level. As I stood there, signaling during practice, I watched as the defensive players employed ridiculous amounts of effort. Every practice, the players carry a small device in their shoulder pads. The device measures speed and overall physical output. This week's data was the highest it had been all year. Coach Kelly was right. We were prepared, and now it was time to show Clemson all the hard work we had put in.

At the stadium, the team dressed and took the field for warmups. It was a beautiful night—clear, with little wind and temperatures in the low 60s. Warmups were crisp, and the team returned to the locker room for a final dose of inspiration prior to taking the field. In his pregame remarks, Kelly reiterated his themes from the hotel and reassured the team that if they simply played to the level that they were capable, good things would happen. Following Kelly's speech and as they prepared to take the field, Father Nate led them through the Our Father. It finished, as it always does, with a plea to Mary:

> Our Lady, Queen of Victory!
> Pray for us!

From there, the team strapped on their helmets and went down the stairs to the tunnel. Each player slapped the PLAY LIKE A CHAMPION TODAY sign on their way down, and the players gathered in the shadows one last time before taking the field.

Then, after weeks, months, and perhaps years of anticipation, at 7:37 PM, the No. 4 Notre Dame Fighting Irish burst from the tunnel to the screams of 11,011 eager fans. Soon thereafter, the No. 1 Clemson Tigers, owners of a 28-game conference winning streak and two of the previous four national championships, took the field. As kickoff in this battle of undefeateds drew nearer, fifth-year senior defensive end Daelin Hayes walked alone to midfield to represent his team at the opening coin flip. The Irish won, and following their choice to receive the opening kickoff, the Notre Dame kick-return team took the field as "Here Come the Irish" rang over the loudspeakers. This was it—this game had been circled on the schedule since Clemson had bested the Irish in Arlington, Texas, on December 29, 2018, and after months of chaos and uncertainty, the day had finally arrived.

Clemson kicker B.T. Potter booted the ball out the back of the end zone, and the Irish offense began at the 25-yard line. On the first play—an eight-yard completion to senior tight end Brock Wright—a holding penalty on the Tigers improved Notre Dame's position to first-and-10 from their own 35. There, Ian Book handed to running back Kyren Williams, who worked patiently toward the Clemson sideline before finding a hole and racing 65 yards for a touchdown—leaving more than one Tigers defender grasping at thin air in the process. After a Jonathan Doerer extra point, the Irish found themselves leading 7–0 just 33 seconds into the contest. The Irish couldn't have drawn their start up any better, and Notre Dame Stadium roared with excitement as the defense prepared to take the field.

REED: A ridiculous run and powerful momentum for the rest of the game. The run gave me flashbacks to a Dexter Williams run against Stanford my sophomore year. Coming off a team suspension, Dexter made a promise to a group of us. He said something to the effect of, "I done waited long enough. First carry, I'm taking that baby to the crib." Lo and behold, the first time Dex touched the ball, he ran it 45 yards for a Fighting Irish touchdown. The sideline was absolute chaos. "He did it! He did it!" Kyren's run evoked an eerily similar response. Jumping and screaming, the sideline was overcome with joy and hope for the rest of the game.

JOHN: It was an absolutely incredible run, and I'll never forget the chaos on the sideline immediately after it happened. I've been there for some pretty incredible plays in my time at ND, but that one has to be near the top of the list. And though Kyren deserves a tremendous amount of credit, of course, the offensive line was absolutely outstanding there as well. The left side of Clemson's defensive line slanted toward the middle of the field, and Banks did an unbelievable job of sealing off the nose guard, which let Liam take the linebacker to open such a big hole for Kyren. I've played scout defense for long enough to know that he doesn't need a whole lot of open space to create serious problems for a defense, and I think the Clemson defense learned that pretty quickly that night.

Following a muffed return on the ensuing kickoff, the Notre Dame kickoff team forced Clemson into a long field by pinning them on their own 12. A holding penalty moved them even further back, and thus the Tigers' drive began at their own 6-yard-line. Following a 10-yard carry on first down, the Irish defense bowed up—stuffing the Tigers in the backfield on third-and-1 to force a punt, which Matthew Salerno returned to the Notre Dame 44. Less than three minutes into the game, the Irish found themselves ahead by a touchdown, with the ball, and on a short field. The offense took the field and, following two unremarkable run plays, Book found fifth-year senior Javon McKinley on a go route for a gain of 28. Suddenly, the Irish found themselves deep in Clemson territory—threatening to take a two-score lead early in the first quarter.

REED: Javon McKinley is one of the most underrated and consistent wide receivers in college football. He's strong as an ox, can catch anything thrown his way, and he knows the game.

JOHN: It was an outstanding throw and catch, to be sure, but what made it all possible was Kyren's blitz pickup. They brought six and sent the linebacker through the left B gap, and he absolutely stoned him.

From there, Notre Dame converted a third down and found themselves with a first-and-10 from the Clemson 11. Two Book carries set up a third-and-3, after which Williams carried the ball to the 2—setting up a fourth-and-less-than-1. Faced with the choice of whether to go for it or take the points, Coach Kelly left the offense on the field, and the Irish aligned in 14 personnel— one running back and four tight ends—signaling to the world that they planned to run right through the Clemson defense. However, a false-start penalty prior to the snap moved the Irish back five yards, forcing the kicking team onto the field. A 24-yard field goal from Doerer sailed through the uprights, and the Irish led 10–0 with just under six minutes to play in the first quarter. And though six would have certainly been better than three on that drive, it was hard to feel anything but positive about Notre Dame's performance thus far. They'd been stout on defense, moved the ball while converting third downs, and asserted themselves in the kicking game. The crowd was engaged, and amid a global pandemic, all was well at Notre Dame Stadium.

Despite what some particularly optimistic Domers may have told you at that point, however, this game was far from over. Uiagalelei led the Tigers offense back onto the field and, rolling to his right on a third-and-2, fired a missile to Joseph Ngata for a first down, giving the Tigers a new set of downs around midfield. On the next play, he connected with Cornell Powell on a post route for a 53-yard touchdown, sending a message to the entire world that this would be a game after all. In fewer than two minutes, Clemson had responded, and the score was now 10–7. The Tigers weren't going anywhere, and it became clear in that instant that this game would be close.

REED: I wouldn't be as bold to say confidence had set in, but the boys were feeling comfortable. An impressive throw from Uiagalelei allowed for a well-earned seven points for Clemson. Nonetheless, the sideline stayed cool, calm, and collected. We knew we could play with these guys, and we weren't about to let a minor setback get in our way.

JOHN: To their credit, it was a great play call—we were playing Cover 4, and they did an excellent job of pulling our safety down and toward the middle of the field by releasing the slot player inside. It created space over the top, and he put it on the money where only his guy could catch it. That pass was when I really began to appreciate Uiagalelei's arm talent—it seemed like he just flicked his wrist, and it was on a line 40 yards downfield. After a pretty euphoric first 10 minutes, it was certainly a reminder of just how dangerous these guys were, as well as the performance it was going to take to beat them.

Following another B.T. Potter touchback, the Irish began another drive with just over four minutes to play in the first quarter. Successive third-down completions to Ben Skowronek and Tommy Tremble situated the Irish in Clemson territory. From there a 14-yard, first-down completion to McKinley again had them in scoring position as the first quarter drew to a close. The Notre Dame offense had been very efficient thus far and, on its third drive of the game, it appeared to be heading toward yet another scoring opportunity. It was a far cry from its three-point performance in Arlington just two years earlier, and any questions about our offense's ability to move the ball against the Brent Venables–engineered Clemson defense had so far been put to rest.

A hard-fought second-down carry from Kyren Williams earned the Irish a first-and-goal from the 10, but incompletions on second and third down again forced the kicking team onto the field. Doerer connected on a 27-yarder, and the Irish now led 13–7. Though they had again fallen short of paydirt, they'd moved the ball 66 yards, recorded four first downs, and taken more than six minutes off the clock. All week, the staff had reinforced that ball control and time of possession—always relevant metrics in football—were paramount in a matchup like this. With that in mind, there was a lot to feel good about on the Notre Dame sideline—even though they hadn't finished the last two drives the way they had hoped.

JOHN: It's one thing to have success with big plays, but at some point, you have to be able to sustain drives. Though we'd come up short in the red zone thus far, our proficiency on third down was reassuring as we made our stretch run in the first half. It wasn't just that we were converting—it was the way we were doing it. Between the hard-fought yards on the ground and the contested catches our guys seemed to keep coming down with, it became increasingly clear that the success we'd had so far was no accident. We could play with these guys, and we knew it.

On the ensuing kickoff, the Tigers looked to spark a drive like the one they'd just completed by sending two-time ACC Player of the Year Travis Etienne out to handle return duties. Down two scores the week prior against Boston College, they'd done the same thing to open the second half, and the Irish coverage unit knew that Clemson was hoping that Etienne could put their offense on a short field. However, a booming kick by Doerer forced him to backtrack, and he ultimately caught the ball a yard deep in his own end zone. Undeterred, he took it out anyway— and was almost instantly met by linebacker Jack Lamb, who beat a block and made a remarkable solo tackle at the Clemson 12. Once again, the Tigers were forced to begin their drive with field position stacked against them.

REED: This seems like another place for me to subtly brag about my linebacker core. With our linebacker group's profound depth, special teams was an obvious place for the non-starters to display their ability. Bo Bauer and Jack Lamb were the tip of the spear when it came to special teams. Their dominance was so powerful, teams were forced to change their plans mid-game. And fortunately for them, they were followed closely by able-bodied sophomores JD Bertrand and Jack Kiser. Our coordinator utilized as many linebackers as he could in every phase of special teams.

JOHN: All week in meetings, we'd been told that they would only put Etienne out there to return kicks when they knew they needed a big play. To see them make that choice so quickly and pin them deep in their own territory anyway was yet another big momentum boost for us early in the game.

Despite their less-than-ideal start, however, the Clemson offense again demonstrated their explosiveness, as Uiagalelei connected with Amari Rodgers on consecutive second-down completions of 27 and 35 yards to bring the Tigers deep into Notre Dame territory. Neither completion was a particularly long throw. Both were short passes designed to get the eventual Biletnikoff Award semifinalist in open space, and they worked almost to perfection. In the blink of an eye, it seemed, the Tigers were threatening to tie the game.

> **REED:** The success of these plays alarmed Lea. So much so that we wrote up these plays multiple times during practice in the later weeks. The largely walk-on-led scout offense did an exceptional job preparing our starting defense for Clemson. Greg Mailey and Matt Salerno performed admirably in their attempts to capture the talents of college football's top receivers.

> **JOHN:** He might have broken or evaded four tackles on that first catch, and I distinctly remember how upset Coach Kelly was on the headset. Everyone—players, coaches, and fans alike—know that you can't allow yards after the catch like that, but it's not until you see it up close like Reed and I did that you really appreciate how difficult it is to bring a guy like that down when he has room to work.

After a tackle for loss following a well-timed blitz from safety Kyle Hamilton and a Clemson incompletion, the Irish defense had forced a third-and-12—an opportunity to get off the field after allowing two big plays to start the drive. However, Uiagalelei evaded pressure and again found Rodgers to move the chains and bring the Tigers into the Notre Dame red zone. Run plays on first and second down set up a third-and-5, where an A-gap blitz from Bo Bauer forced an incompletion and brought the Clemson kicking team onto the field to attempt a 25-yard field goal. Potter easily completed the kick to cut the margin to three, but not before the NBC broadcast was moved to USA Network to accommodate then president-elect Biden's acceptance speech. Those in the stadium in South Bend had no idea, of course, but to all those watching across the country, it was yet another reminder of the craziness of the weeks and months prior.

Following yet another touchback on a B.T. Potter kickoff, the Irish began with the ball at the 25, eager to build on their success from the three previous drives. Following a 13-yard completion to Skowronek, however, the drive stalled. A sack on first down left them substantially behind the chains, and a false start on third-and-12 placed Book and the offense in a difficult position. An incompletion brought Jay Bramblett and the Notre Dame punt team onto the field for the first time that evening. His 38-yard punt was fair caught at the Clemson 31, and the Tigers offense returned to the field down three but with more momentum than they'd had at any point thus far. It was their best starting field position yet, and suddenly, they had the opportunity to drive down the field to take a lead for the first time that night. The Irish—after such a dominant first quarter—were on their heels.

Enter Jeremiah Owusu-Koramoah—Notre Dame's unanimous All-America linebacker. In what may have been the play of the season, he blitzed from his rover position and intercepted a fumbled pitch from Uiagalelei to Etienne. From there, he raced 23 yards to the end zone, extending the Irish's lead to 10 and firmly placing them back in the driver's seat of this contest. It was a play that few others could have made. As the ball was snapped, he sprinted from his pre-snap alignment over the slot receiver and evaded the pulling guard as he shot the D-gap, putting himself in perfect position to make a play. Once he got there, the ball seemed to fall perfectly into his hands. From there, he simply ran away from Etienne—undoubtedly one of the fastest players in the ACC, if not the country—to the end zone.

JOHN: Any time we get word that Wu is coming on a blitz, there's some excitement among the signalers on the sideline—and though we've seen him make some pretty incredible plays through the years, this one might have been his magnum opus. It was perfectly executed from start to finish, and it provided a spark that we so desperately needed at that point. It happened so fast, but once everyone realized what was happening, the sideline went absolutely bonkers. You can ask Coach Lea, but I think I may have jumped 11 feet in the air once he crossed the goal line.

REED: I spoke with Coach Lea about this play after the game. He was curious as to why I wasn't as excited as John. On film, John was going absolutely bonkers. Jokingly, I told him I just wasn't surprised. I knew the play, I sent in the signal, and I practiced with Wu and the Rovers every day. I knew Wu would be right on Etienne from the start. The touchdown was textbook.

Following the extra point by Doerer, the Irish lined up to kick off. The coverage team again pinned the Tigers deep in their own territory, and Uiagalelei led the Clemson offense out to begin the drive from their own 15-yard line. There was just under six minutes to play in the first half, and the momentum was undoubtedly back on Notre Dame's side. Following a short carry by Etienne and an incompletion, the Tigers faced another third-and-long. True to form, Uiagalelei found Rodgers on a slant route over the middle, clearly past the first-down marker, and for an instant it appeared that the drive would continue. However, Owusu-Koramoah again made a game-changing play—reaching across Rodgers' body to strip the ball and force a fumble that was recovered by cornerback Nick McCloud. Though the play was reviewed, it was ultimately determined that he had, in fact, made a "football move" prior to being stripped, and the call on the field stood. The defense had come through with a big play again, and the Irish offense now found themselves deep in Clemson territory with an opportunity to take a three-score lead.

> **JOHN:** We did a "ball disruption" circuit at least once a week in practice, and it clearly paid dividends that night. Winning the turnover battle is critical in a game like that one, and I truly believe that it was the work the defense did on Tuesdays and Wednesdays throughout the year that set us up for success in situations like that.

However, the next drive was almost over before it began, as a penalty for an illegal blind-side block on first down moved the Irish back to the Clemson 40. A third-down completion to Tremble wasn't enough to move the chains, and the field-goal team was again tasked with extending the Irish lead. Following a Clemson timeout, Doerer's 45-yard kick sailed through the uprights. He remained perfect on the day, and Notre Dame now led 23–10 with 2:41 remaining in the first half.

This time around, rather than try his luck against the Notre Dame coverage unit, Etienne opted to fair catch Doerer's kick-off—allowing Clemson the opportunity to begin their drive at their own 25. With under three minutes to play and just two timeouts, time was a consideration for the Tigers—at least initially. Successive 20-plus-yard completions from Uiagalelei to Braden Galloway and Etienne, however, put them within striking distance with approximately two minutes to play. As they had done all night, though, the Irish defense firmed up—stopping Etienne in the backfield on a first-down run play, then forcing two consecutive incompletions to bring up fourth down from the Notre Dame 28. Potter remained perfect on the day, cutting Clemson's deficit to 10. For all the offensive fireworks in the first quarter, the second quarter had turned into something of a kickers' duel.

With 1:09 to play, Clemson kicked off to the Irish, who used a series of Ian Book carries to get to the fringe of Doerer's range. Kelly took his final timeout with just three seconds to play and sent his kicking team out to try a 57-yard field goal, while the Tigers sent Etienne back to potentially return the kick if possible. The snap and hold were perfect, and the kick was on target but fell a couple yards short, giving Etienne the opportunity to bring it out. For a few moments, it appeared that he might get free, which would have been an absolutely disastrous turn of events for a Notre Dame team protecting a 10-point lead. As he sped past the first line of tacklers, visions of the 2013 Iron Bowl flashed into the heads of Domers nationwide. Fortunately for the Irish, however, Bramblett—who also served as the holder—was able to bring him down, averting a crisis and preserving Notre Dame's advantage into halftime.

REED: People have laughed when I've said this, but I firmly believe that that was the biggest play of the season. There was no one behind Jay, and we had never practiced tackling with our field-goal team. If it weren't for Jay's body-sacrificing tackle, Etienne would have scored, and the game could have ended very differently. Outstanding awareness on Jay's part.

JOHN: I don't know why, but I had turned around for a second and lost vision of what was going on. I heard Reed start yelling about what a great play Jay made, and—not having seen it—I didn't really understand how remarkable that tackle was. For some reason, I guess I assumed that we would get him on the ground and head into halftime up 10. It was only later that I really gained an appreciation for what Jay did.

Both teams returned to their locker rooms to refuel and discuss their second-half adjustments. Before returning to the field, Coach Kelly emphasized the importance of the next defensive possession. A stop to start the second half, he said, would be critical to his team's chances to ultimately win the game. Of course, this would be easier said than done. Clemson was renowned as a second-half team. They had a number of impressive comebacks under their belt, perhaps the most notable of which occurred in the previous year's Fiesta Bowl. And just a week before, Clemson had been down two scores to Boston College and—following a long kickoff return from Etienne—had surged past the Eagles to a 34–28 victory. The first half had shown that the Tigers could move the ball quickly, and both sides anticipated a hard-fought second half.

Following a kick out of bounds to start the second half, Clemson began their drive at their own 35-yard line. Immediately, the Tigers took to the air. Another third-down completion to Rodgers brought them past midfield, where—after an incompletion— an 11-yard strike to Powell got them to the Notre Dame 30.

Threatened yet again by the explosive Tigers offense, the Irish defense buckled down, stopping Etienne for a short gain on first down and pressuring Uiagalelei into two consecutive incompletions. On fourth-and-9, Potter connected from 46 yards—his third field goal of the night—to cut the Tigers' deficit to just seven points. Now leading 23–16, the Irish offense, intent on stretching their lead back to two scores, prepared to take the field.

However, after another touchback, the Notre Dame offense stalled. A negative play on first down left them behind the chains, and despite a seven-yard gain by Kyren Williams on second down, they were unable to convert on third down. On fourth down, a short punt from Bramblett was downed at the Clemson 40. With 10:41 left to play in the third quarter, the Tigers found themselves just 60 yards from tying the game.

From there, the Clemson offense moved down the field with almost surgical efficiency. Uiagalelei completed seven of his eight pass attempts and converted a designed run on a critical fourth-and-inches to earn the Tigers a first-and-goal. Two plays later, he found tight end Davis Allen in the end zone on a play-action pass, leaving just an extra point between the Tigers and the Irish. Potter remained perfect on the day, and suddenly the game was tied. Notre Dame Stadium, which had been so full of energy in the first half, fell quiet. To a Notre Dame football pessimist, this was an all-too-familiar tale—a promising start against a talented, favored opponent that couldn't be sustained as the second half wore on.

However, this wasn't 2019 in Athens, Georgia. Nor was it 2017 or 2015 in Palo Alto, California. This team was different—and, for the first time in a long time, the Irish were on their home turf for a marquee game like this. On the first play from scrimmage, Book identified single coverage and connected with McKinley on a post route for a 45-yard gain right over the top of the Tigers defense. Following their anemic performance on the previous drive, the Irish offense was back in business, and they'd again proven that they were every bit as worthy to be on this stage as the Tigers were.

> **REED:** I said it before and I'll say it again. Javon McKinley. Underrated.

> **JOHN:** Throughout the game, we had guys come up big in moments where we needed them the most, and this play was no exception. When you watch the replay, it's that much more impressive—he dove, flipped the ball up to himself, and secured it through the ground. After a rough start to the third quarter, it was exactly what we needed—particularly in the sense that I think it proved to Clemson that they were still in for a dogfight.

A third-down completion to freshman Michael Mayer brought the Irish into the red zone with around 2:30 to play in the third quarter. Carries by Book and Williams left them with a third-and-short from the Clemson 6. After having settled for field goals three times already, Notre Dame knew they needed a touchdown to wrest control of this game back. They aligned with three receivers to the field and a tight end to the boundary, and Book carried the ball toward the short side of the field. He gained more than enough for the first down but was tackled by linebacker Jake Venables, who was able to pry the ball loose before Book's knee touched the ground. The ball skittered into the end zone, where the Tigers recovered. A promising drive for the Irish ended in no points, and a golden opportunity had been squandered. With under a minute to play in the third quarter, Clemson took over on their own 20 with the game still tied.

The Tigers sought to capitalize on their good fortune and repeat the success of their previous drive by handing to Etienne, who gained five yards on first down—setting up a second-and-5. A two-yard gain brought up third down and, in the face of pressure from the Irish defensive line, Uiagalelei again targeted Rodgers as time expired in the third quarter. His pass was broken up by linebacker Shayne Simon, and the Notre Dame defense had earned a stop—again coming through when the team needed it most.

> **JOHN:** At that point, I was absolutely certain that we were going to win the game. Clemson beats teams by forcing them to make mistakes down the stretch, then capitalizing on those mistakes to put opponents away for good. Once we got that stop, it felt like we took their best punch and were still left standing. I've heard it said that if an intimidator is unable to intimidate, he becomes intimidated, and I certainly think this became the case later that evening.
>
> In the weight room and on the practice field, we are often confronted with "sudden change" scenarios that force us to adapt to uncertain, adverse circumstances. It wasn't any fun when that meant laps around Loftus early in the morning, but I truly believe it was those sorts of experiences that prepared the team for situations like that.

The fourth quarter began with a Clemson punt, fair caught by Salerno at the Notre Dame 28. A penalty for fair catch interference moved the Irish ahead 15 yards, so our drive began at the 43. A 29-yard catch-and-run by Mayer moved us into opposing territory, where the drive ultimately stalled. On fourth-and-7, Doerer connected on his fourth field goal of the day—a 44-yarder from the left hash—to break the tie and push the Irish ahead. With

11:37 to play in regulation, just three points separated the two teams.

Following an Etienne return, the Clemson offense responded with another explosive play of its own—a 51-yard bomb from Uiagalelei to Powell that put them in the red zone. The Irish defense was on its heels as the Tigers threatened to take their first lead of the night. Again, however, our defense firmed up when it needed to most. Uiagalelei was unable to connect with Rodgers on third down, and the Clemson kicking team took the field in an attempt to even the score once more. From 30 yards out, Potter remained perfect, and the score was knotted at 26 with just under 10 minutes to play.

> **REED:** In the red zone, the offense is limited vertically. There is no option for a deep pass due to the lack of field space. Knowing this gives the defense one less thing to worry about and less area to cover. Most passing routes would cut across, horizontally, to the other side of the field. Lea built red-zone defense into our weekly practice schedule. We practiced circumstances where we are backed up past our own 20-yard line every Attention to Detail Thursday.

> **JOHN:** Red-zone defense had been an emphasis for us all year, and—as Reed has mentioned before—Coach Lea introduced a metric called "RBI Defense" that helped us set targets and measure our progress. It awards the defense points for the points they *prevent* in the red zone (four for a field goal and seven for no score), and keeping a team to three points is considered a victory for us. Obviously, in that situation, it was huge that we were able to keep them from taking the lead.

On the ensuing drive, three straight incompletions forced a Notre Dame punt, which was fair caught at the Clemson 26. From there, the Tigers put together a 12-play, 74-yard touchdown drive that took almost six minutes off the clock, leaving the Irish in a precarious position—behind by a touchdown with less than four minutes to play. After another Potter touchback, the Irish offense rattled off two quick first downs on completions to Mayer and Avery Davis. At midfield with just under three minutes to play, Book and the Notre Dame offense hoped to reach paydirt and tie the game. Following a short completion to Mayer on second down, Book targeted Skowronek on a comeback route. The pass fell incomplete, but flags flew as it appeared the Clemson defensive back may have been too handsy before the ball arrived. Clemson head coach Dabo Swinney was irate—so much so that the officials ultimately announced that there was no foul on the play. The Irish faithful were incensed, but that didn't change the fact that their offense now faced a critical fourth-and-7. Kelly left his offense on the field, and Book again targeted Skowronek, who was open but was unable to haul it in—turning the ball over on downs with 2:10 left on the clock.

With three timeouts, however, Notre Dame wasn't out of the game yet. After stopping Etienne for a loss on second down, Clemson faced third-and-14. A completion to Etienne wasn't enough to move the chains, and the Tigers punt team was forced to take the field. The Irish would get another chance after all, though they would have less than two minutes to go the full length of the field. Salerno fair caught the Tigers punt at the Notre Dame 9, and the offense took the field for what would almost certainly be their last opportunity to tie the game.

On the first play from scrimmage, Book connected with McKinley for a 10-yard gain—stopping the clock to allow the chains to move. On the following play, Book scrambled for another nine yards, smartly maneuvering out of bounds to preserve clock. A second-down pass to Mayer was broken up, but a third-down carry by Williams was more than enough for a first down for the Irish offense—who now sat on their own 43 with 1:14 to play. As Notre Dame aligned with four receivers split out, the Tigers showed double A-gap pressure—meaning that there would likely be single coverage somewhere. With time to throw, Book found it—hitting Davis over the middle of the field for a gain of 53 yards. Suddenly, Notre Dame was knocking on the door. Just four yards stood between them and the six points that would essentially tie the game.

> **JOHN:** The underneath route pulled the backside safety down and away from the middle of the field, and Avery ran an unbelievable route to get open. That's a guy who overcame pretty significant adversity—changing positions more than once—to get to where he is, and nobody deserves the success they've achieved more than he does. It was awesome to see him excel like that, and his performance couldn't have come at a better time for us.

Incompletions on first and second down left the Irish with a third-and-goal from the 4. Book escaped the pocket soon after the snap and, rolling right, found Davis in the end zone to bring Notre Dame to within a point. Replay confirmed what every observer already knew, and following an unnecessarily long delay, Doerer's extra point sailed through the uprights to tie the score at 33–33. Etienne returned the kickoff to the 27, and the Clemson offense took the field and proceeded to take a knee—sending the game to overtime. The Irish hadn't been in an overtime game since 2016, when they lost a heartbreaker to Texas. Though the vast majority of the players on the field that night hadn't been present for that, they nevertheless sought a different outcome than the one the Irish experienced that night in Austin.

Hayes again represented Notre Dame at the coin flip, and was again victorious. The Irish chose to play defense first, forcing the Tigers to begin on offense. Uiagalelei wasted no time, showing play-action then firing a strike to Powell—who fought through multiple tackles on his way to the end zone. Just as overtime had started, it seemed, Clemson had already established a decisive advantage. Following yet another time-consuming review, the ruling on the field was upheld. A Potter extra point pushed the lead to seven, and the stage was set—Notre Dame's hopes of pulling off the upset fell squarely on the shoulders of Book and the offense.

JOHN: The review felt like it took forever, which provided some time for contemplation on the sideline. As the coaches discussed what went wrong, I couldn't help but think about what a shame it would be to have come all this way with nothing to show for ourselves. I had nothing but the utmost confidence in the offense, but that play left a bad taste in everyone's mouth. In football, too much time to think is never a good thing, so I was glad when the ruling was confirmed and the game started back up.

REED: As the defense sat back down in their position groups' allotted circle of chairs, I saw more than a few heads hanging low. We needed a pick-me-up, and it came in the form of Drew White. Drew rose from his chair and walked around the defense, slapping his teammates on the back. He ensured us the offense would score, and when they did, we'd better be ready. Heads rose, and motivation set back in. Drew brought the inspiration the sideline needed at that moment—a real act of leadership.

The Irish began their drive by handing to Williams, who gained two yards. On the following play, Book evaded pressure and found Mayer along the right side for a gain of 15. On first-and-goal from the 8, Book completed another pass to McKinley, which brought them down to the 3. From there, the Irish aligned with five wide receivers split out, then shifted to a formation that positioned Williams in the backfield with three tight ends to the field. Behind the added strength, Williams muscled in from three yards out, leaving an extra point between these two teams and another overtime period. Doerer connected, and the Irish offense headed to the other end of the field to begin the second overtime.

Notre Dame began their drive by handing to Williams, who was stopped in the backfield for a loss of one. On the following play, a designed run by Book brought the offense to the 2-yard line, but the play was called back due to a holding penalty. Fortunately, at the end of the same play, a personal foul on the Tigers gave the Irish a fresh set of downs at the 20. A first-down handoff to Williams led to another negative play, and Notre Dame found itself again behind the chains early in the series. However, a 12-yard scramble by Book on the following play brought up third-and-short. From the 13, Book found Skowronek for a gain of 10—giving the Irish a first-and-goal from the 3. Williams carried for no gain on first down, but offensive coordinator Tommy Rees was undeterred. He called Williams' number again on second down, and he charged in—knocking the Clemson safety back as he crossed the goal line—to give the Irish a 46–40 lead. Doerer connected on the extra point, and Notre Dame was clearly in the driver's seat of this one.

JOHN: Kyren made a statement on that touchdown run. Our resilience on the last couple of drives—overcoming the initial deficit, coming back from negative plays, and working through penalties—gave me a sense that we had them close to a breaking point. When we took the lead, my premonition was absolutely confirmed.

REED: A sigh of relief came over the defensive channel on the headsets. We had our chance. It was our time to strike. Lea consulted with Coach Elston, inquiring as to which defensive front would open up Clemson's offensive line and pressure the young Uiagalelei most. From the sound of it, they wanted to give him no time to think and make him as uncomfortable as possible. At this point, I'm sure it's an easy guess as to who we wanted to blitz...

Now, with *their* backs against the wall, the Clemson offense took the field. Intent on preserving their 36-game regular-season winning streak, they had no choice but to score a touchdown on this drive. The Irish defense, however—energized and inspired by a crowd already working its way toward the field—had other ideas. On first down, defensive end Ade Ogundeji and Owusu-Koramoah met up in the backfield to sack Uiagalelei, leaving the Tigers with a second-and-19. On second down, it was Hayes' turn—he sacked Uiagalelei for a loss of another five, and Clemson now faced third-and-24. Safety Shaun Crawford broke up the third-down pass, and the Irish were suddenly one play from victory. The Tigers took a timeout to regroup as Notre Dame Stadium worked itself into a frenzy.

JOHN: From the field during the timeout, you could see that the students had completely disregarded social distancing and were crowding around the railings nearest the field. There was such electricity in the air that you knew the ushers would be totally powerless to stop what was hopefully coming next.

REED: I waved the players over to the sideline, signaling a time-out. They ran over to huddle with their position coaches. Yes, Coach O'Leary talked about scheme, but the adrenaline rushing through the players made it difficult for them to focus. I've never seen our guys so eager to get back on the field. It reached a point where the coach's main message morphed from a strategic plan to just going out there and giving it all you got. We had them backed up pretty far—what we needed right now was burning passion and disciplined aggression.

On fourth-and-24, the Irish rushed just three—leaving eight back in coverage. Uiagalelei threw to Allen, who was well short of the line to gain as he attempted to pitch the ball back to his teammate. After a few brief moments of chaos, it became clear that cornerback Nick McCloud had recovered the ball. The game was over. The Irish had knocked off the No. 1 Tigers, 47–40.

JOHN: From where we were standing, it was tough to see exactly what had happened. I saw him pitch the ball back and couldn't help but think of the play Rutgers had made the week before—completing what seemed like a dozen laterals on the way to an improbable touchdown. Once I was sure that that hadn't happened, I sprinted onto the field with everyone else—actually losing my headset in the process.

REED: I've never sprinted so fast. My heart was racing as I ran out to meet the defense on the field. Within seconds the entire team was celebrating between the hashes on the 30-yard line. Tears flowed, teammates embraced, and smiles spread from ear to ear.

Following McCloud's recovery, Notre Dame Stadium erupted into utter pandemonium. Amid a global pandemic, students stormed the field for the first time since 1993. It was green as far as the eye could see, and it seemed like every inch of turf was covered with fans.

JOHN: We'd been instructed to leave the field as soon as the game was over, but there was no chance I was going to do that. As the students stormed the field, I found myself at the bottom of what felt like a mosh pit. Normally, that's something that would bother me, but I was too excited to even care. I saw friends everywhere I looked, and it was only then that the gravity of what we'd just done resonated with me. Otherwise stoic college students were crying tears of joy, and I found my cousin—who was visiting for the weekend—on the field. People who otherwise didn't know one another came together over this shared experience, and I realized that this was more than just a big win—this was a moment that would forever be a part of Notre Dame history. I think I was the last one of the players on the field, and I sang the alma mater with my cousin, as well as my friend's parents, before they had to physically drag me up the tunnel.

REED: As the students surrounded me, I thought back to where my friends were sitting. I swam through a sea of cheering fans to where I thought they would have run in. Out of the chaos, I spotted my brother Harry who was visiting for the game. I gave him a huge hug and laughed with him until my roommates found us as well. Similar to John, I paid little attention to the loudspeaker, informing all players to head back inside immediately. This was not a moment I was going to miss. Eventually, one of our graduate assistants called me out and pointed toward the tunnel. Begrudgingly, I followed orders. As I was weaving my way back to the locker room, I was hugged by random students overcome with emotion. I chuckled, hugged them back, and continued through the maze. It was an experience like no other and a feeling I will never forget.

Back in the locker room, the celebration continued. The Irish had now won 23 consecutive games at home, but none of the previous 22 had felt as sweet as this. Book received the game ball after a 310-yard performance, and Coach Kelly's speech congratulated the team on their accomplishment, while reminding them that there was still a lot for the group still to achieve. He urged the team to be safe, and the 2020 Irish sang the fight song with more gusto than they ever had before. Furthermore, as the players left the locker room, they saw that many of the students still hadn't left. The tunnel leading to the field was full of screaming fans, who continued to congratulate the players as they went to find their families.

Long after the game had finished, there wasn't much appetite for sleep among students in South Bend. Wanting to soak up every last bit of excitement from the day's events, students gathered in a parking lot outside Legacy Village, a housing complex east of campus. Hugs were shared, music was played, and a group of kids whose lives had changed dramatically in the past several months simply enjoyed one another's company until the wee hours of the morning. Nobody wanted to leave, and for a few hours, the only thing that mattered was the here and now.

REED: It was one of the happiest days of my life. I was surrounded by the people I love and the friends I'll have forever. The time had little effect on our celebration and we didn't need much either. One speaker and parking lot floodlight was enough for a rowdy group of college friends and teammates to have the night of their lives.

JOHN: It might not have been the smartest thing we'd ever done, given the state of public health at the time and everything, but that gathering was something I'll never forget. To see the joy it brought everyone on campus and know that I played a small role in making that happen was one of the most rewarding feelings I've ever experienced. It's truly something that the Class of '21 will talk about forever.

Much to the chagrin of the early-morning revelers in South Bend, however, the sun rose on the morning of November 8. And though spirits were still sky-high from the previous day's victory, it would soon be time for the Irish to turn their focus to the next week's opponent—one that, interestingly enough, had a history of taking down the Irish in the wake of some of their most triumphant moments.

CHAPTER 8

SHIPPING UP TO BOSTON

Most die-hard **Notre Dame** football fans cringe at the mere mention of 1993. It was a year that included an extended period of dominance, a timeless triumph, and a painful defeat that still reminds Irish fans of what might have been. Even today, 1993 undoubtedly occupies a complicated place in Irish fans' collective memories. For those who are unaware of that year's sad tale, here's a quick flashback. On November 13, 1993, the Lou Holtz–led Fighting Irish took on the No. 1–ranked Florida State Seminoles. This previous "Game of the Century" took place on the hallowed grounds of Notre Dame Stadium. This contest marked the first-ever recording of ESPN's *College GameDay,* which has traveled to college football's greatest matchups ever since. Eventual Heisman Trophy winner Charlie Ward was the Seminoles' quarterback at the time, and their roster included future NFL stars Derrick Brooks and Warrick Dunn—among others. With head coach Bobby Bowden at the helm, the Seminoles brought an undefeated record to South Bend, setting up a matchup of unbeatens. Both schools had romped through their schedules up to that point, and it was No. 1 vs. No 2. In an era before the BCS or the College Football Playoff, it wasn't a huge stretch to assume that the winner of this skirmish would have the inside track on that season's national championship.

Using the friendly home crowd to their advantage, the Irish dominated the game's start and took a comfortable fourth-quarter lead with the score at 31–17. Ward, however, was not going to give up that easy. A series of dominant drives turned a game the Irish thought they had in the bag into an unnervingly close one. With a few seconds left on the clock and the score tightened to 31–24, the Seminoles had the ball on the Irish 14. Ward dropped back to pass on the final play and let it loose. Notre Dame's Shawn Wooden broke up the pass and saved the day. Celebration ensued, and the Fighting Irish sat atop the polls the following week.

Spirits were extremely high heading into next week's matchup against the 17th-ranked Boston College Eagles. A win against BC would likely launch the Irish into the Fiesta Bowl, giving them a shot to play for the national championship. However, at 7–2, the Tom Coughlin–coached Eagles had nothing to lose and were prepared to give everything they had to beat Notre Dame. Empowered by their status as underdogs, Boston College started hot. They led 10–0 at the end of the first quarter and 24–10 at the half. In the fourth quarter, the Irish were down 38–17. It was at this point that the Irish found their stride. Quarterback Kevin McDougal gradually chipped away at Boston College's lead, series by series. In the final 11 minutes of the game, the Irish racked up 22 points, giving them the lead at 39–38. Victory was in sight, and the miraculous comeback was almost complete. Boston College had the ball on their 25-yard line with a little over a minute left. If Notre Dame could get one stop, the game was theirs. Linebacker Pete Bercich had that chance, but the game-clinching interception slipped through his fingers. Boston College's quarterback Glen Foley guided the Eagles down the field, passing four times, three to tight end Pete Mitchell and once more to wide receiver Ivan

Boyd. They were in field-goal range. David Gordon lined up his kick from 41 yards out. Despite the cries of a raucous home crowd in South Bend, he connected—winning the game for the Eagles. Thousands of hearts dropped nationwide as the ball soared through the uprights.

Though they'd defeated the Seminoles the week before, the Irish were effectively forced out of national championship contention. A victory over Texas A&M in the Cotton Bowl didn't do enough to convince the voters otherwise, and the title was awarded to Florida State—who had defeated Nebraska in the Orange Bowl.

> **JOHN:** I didn't necessarily grow up a Notre Dame fan, so I wasn't familiar with the story of the 1993 team until I arrived on campus. As far as should-have-beens are concerned, there isn't one that seems to hurt Irish loyalists more than the '93 squad—who many say was more talented, top to bottom, than the 1988 national championship team. With that in mind, the parallels were almost too obvious. You treat every opponent the same, but the guys were certainly aware of that narrative heading into our trip to Chestnut Hill.

As the only two Catholic schools that play FBS football, logic would suggest that there should be a natural rivalry between Notre Dame and BC. They share a common patrimony—legendary coach Frank Leahy had won national championships at both schools. Yet, though the two academic institutions had long viewed each other as peers and counterparts, there had been surprisingly little engagement on the gridiron for much of the 20th century. In fact, prior to 1993, the two teams had met just four times. The Irish were 4–0 in those games, making a genuine rivalry difficult to establish. However, that fateful afternoon in 1993 changed everything. The Eagles' win was featured on the cover of *Sports Illustrated* the following week, and the Irish faithful were left to wonder about what could have been. Today, the matchup between the two schools was referred to as the "Holy War," and the winner goes home with the Frank Leahy Memorial trophy— one of six that the Irish play for. The vagaries of the scheduling arrangement that season, however, made this the only traveling trophy on the line for the Irish that season—a fact not lost on Coach Kelly, a Boston native. During the week, he made one thing clear: the trophy would be returning to South Bend on the same plane on which it traveled to Boston.

REED: Having just knocked off No. 1-ranked Clemson at home, this story loomed heavy in many players' minds. Conversely, I'm sure the coaches at Boston College used this story to motivate their players for the game ahead. Additionally, the Eagles had formed a wonderful tradition honoring a past alumnus that landed on this year's game. Their annual "Red Bandana" game honored Welles Crowther, a former Boston College lacrosse player who saved multiple lives during the 9/11 attacks. Welles used a red bandana to protect his face from the smoke and rubble. He saved 18 people's lives before losing his life. An unbelievable tradition that we greatly respected. Needless to say, we knew morale would be high on the Eagles sideline.

On November 14, the Irish traveled through Chestnut Hill, Massachusetts, passing the windy reservoir and arriving at Alumni Stadium on a crisp Boston evening. As we filed out of the buses, they were directed through the open stadium gates toward the locker room. Due to social distancing, as was the case at many travel game locations, the visitors' locker room was not large enough for the entire team to fit, since each player had to be separated by a minimum of one locker. Part of the team was relocated to another room to change and prepare for the afternoon's contest.

REED: The other room that week was the women's restroom located in the stadium's concourse. In a typical year, this would be the bathroom for all the female fans to use during the game. This year, Alumni Stadium was utterly bare, allowing the room to be used by the team's "most special" players. The women's restroom was locker room to seven players. All of whom were walk-ons, myself and John included. We walked into the sight of seven seats leaned up against the bathroom sinks, with our uniforms and gear hanging off stall doors closest to our chair—a wonderful sight to behold. We laughed at the ridiculous circumstances this pandemic had brought.

JOHN: As the select few of us chosen to dress in the women's bathroom were directed away from the rest of the team to our destination, I had the good fortune of running into ESPN reporter Molly McGrath—who, like most other observers, was both intrigued and amused by our locker arrangement. She asked me what was going on, curious if we were managers or special teams players—both of which were good guesses, given our appearance, stature, and relative athletic ability. Completely awestruck, I somehow had the wherewithal to respond, informing her that we were walk-on signalers—the lowest guys on the totem pole—and that these accommodations were not only serviceable but were actually better than what we were used to. Believe it or not, she laughed, providing me with an entirely unhealthy level of confidence as I got my things together to get ready for the game.

The defensive players laid their bags down next to their "lockers" and headed out to the field, as was tradition for the entire unit before every game. The players linked arms around the BC logo at midfield and prayed. After the prayer, the players huddled together in the middle, where Coach Lea gave his pregame speech as well as his final three things to think about in the minutes before the kickoff. These points typically revolved around guarding individual players, recognizing common schemes and the plays that follow, and having faith in the team's preparation. The players broke the huddle, walked the field, and headed back into the locker room.

> **REED:** Unlike other games this season, our parents and extended family were not allowed to attend. As we broke the huddle, I walked around the logo staring into the stands. They were completely bare, save a handful of posterboard busts of some Boston College students, faculty, and alumni. It was a weird environment to play in, knowing millions of people watched the game on their TVs at home.

> **JOHN:** There might have been 10 NFL scouts in the stands, but that was it. They tried to simulate crowd noise, but the atmosphere felt like a scrimmage. I'd never seen or experienced anything like it.

During warmups, the Irish attempted to adjust to the unusually sterile atmosphere. Music and simulated crowd noise blared over the loudspeaker, but it ultimately failed to simulate a traditional game-day experience. Though playing in front of reduced crowds—as they had all season—was certainly an adjustment, preparing to play a college football game in front of a completely empty stadium was another thing entirely. Before kickoff, Kelly reminded his players that they would need to "provide their own juice," since there was no crowd there to do it for them.

Shaun Crawford represented the Irish at the coin toss, which Boston College won. It elected to defer, giving Notre Dame the ball to start the game. The Eagles kicked off, and the second-ranked Irish got off to a slow but steady start. After a five-minute drive keyed by two Javon McKinley catches, Jon Doerer nailed the ball through the uprights for a hard-earned three points.

Out to an early 3–0 lead, the Irish kickoff unit pinned the Eagles at their own 20, forcing the BC offense to start on a long field. However, a busted coverage and an open gap up the middle allowed for two considerable gains by the Eagles, moving them to the Irish 23 after just three plays from scrimmage. In an attempt to save the drive, safety Shaun Crawford screamed off the edge, sacking former Notre Dame quarterback Phil Jurkovec, bringing up second-and-18. Unfazed, however, the Eagles continued downfield. Following a defensive holding penalty on a critical third down, Jurkovec connected with wide receiver Zay Flowers, in acrobatic fashion, for the Eagles' first touchdown of the day.

> **JOHN:** It was an outstanding throw and catch. We got a rush, but Phil was able to make the throw with a man in his face and find his man. We all respected Phil's talent, and he was making very clear that he was out to make a statement.

Now behind 7–3, the onus was on the Irish offense to respond and regain the lead. However, a fumble on the first play of the drive, deep in Notre Dame territory, gave the ball back to the Eagles. Faced with a critical possession, the Irish defense bowed up. A successful red-zone defensive stand, keyed by a third-down tackle for loss by Bo Bauer and Rylie Mills, held Boston College to a field goal. Notre Dame was down 10–3 and was in desperate need of some offensive productivity.

The next possession, Ian Book escaped the pocket and tossed to Avery Davis for a gain of 22. A series of positive runs and passes brought the Irish to the 10-yard line. From there, Book aired it out to the back right pylon. Ben Skowronek made an incredible catch through the arms of a well-positioned corner. As he clutched the ball, he pulled it over the defender's head and away from trouble. After scoring, Skowronek screamed in the corner's face—earning an unsportsmanlike-conduct penalty—and embraced his teammates.

> **JOHN:** If I was asked for one word to describe Ben Skowronek, it would be, without a sliver of a doubt, *competitive*. The call seemed a little weak to me, but that's beside the point. We needed someone to step up and assert themselves at that point in the game, and though it may have set us back a few yards, that play helped set the tone for the rest of the game.

On the ensuing drive, however, the Eagles proved that it would take more than some garden-variety trash talk to put them away. Phil Jurkovec, in an attempt to beat his former teammates and prove his worth, evaded three Notre Dame linemen and chucked the ball downfield while being crushed by linebacker Bo Bauer. The ball fell into the hands of wide receiver Jaelen Gill for an impressive 34-yard gain. After a first-down carry by Jurkovec, however, the Irish defense held Boston College to a field goal. Again, the Irish found themselves behind, this time by a three-point margin.

> **REED:** Phil Jurkovec was a great guy and an exceptional quarterback who was caught in a challenging position. He wanted to be the starting quarterback and knew Book would be at Notre

Dame for at least another year. He saw the opportunity to start elsewhere and jumped at the chance. Many players are still very close with Phil, and we wish him the best going forward.

JOHN: There wasn't a guy on our sideline that day who didn't—and still doesn't—have tremendous respect for Phil. He's a phenomenal guy who was nothing but an outstanding teammate during his time in South Bend. I was disappointed when he decided to leave, but I'd been glad to see him have success out east that year—until he started doing it against us. It was unfortunate that we got matched up with him due to the schedule change, because it's hard to root against the guy.

Looking to turn the game around, the Irish responded with two quick scoring drives. After a carry that brought the Irish to midfield, Book connected with Avery Davis for 48 yards. Soon after, running back C'Bo Flemister finished off the drive with a two-yard touchdown. The defense bolstered the offense's success with a quick three-and-out. Next possession, the Irish made it down to the Eagles' 13-yard line. Book eluded an aggressive crew of defensive lineman and found Ben Skowronek again for six points. After something of a rocky start, the Irish finally established a healthy lead, 24–13.

Eager to respond, Jurkovec led the Eagles downfield. Another long completion to Gill, this time for 40 yards, put them in field-goal range. At that point, however, the Irish defense stopped the Eagles in their tracks. A pass break-up by Bo Bauer on third down forced head coach Jeff Hafley to settle for three. The 35-yard kick was good, and BC was once again within a score.

After receiving the opening kickoff, the Irish flirted with danger, as Kyren Williams was stripped running up the middle on

the first play of the drive. The Eagles recovered, once again putting their offense on a short field. However, a miscommunication
led to a bad snap by the Eagles' center on third-and-3, giving the
ball right back to Notre Dame. After starting the drive in Boston
College territory, the Irish executed the two-minute drill to perfection. With 10 seconds left in the half and without any timeouts,
Kelly knew he likely had time for one more play before he'd have
to call his field-goal unit onto the field. The ball was snapped, and
Book sailed the ball over the offensive line directly into the hands
of a leaping Ben Skowronek for his third touchdown of the day.
The Fighting Irish headed into the tunnel for halftime, up 31–16.

REED: Yes, we were up by 15, but it sure didn't feel that way. We
knew we weren't playing well. We sat in silence as we waited for
the coaches to come into the locker room. Everyone knew what
was coming. Lea rushed in and walked right over to the linebackers. He brushed right over the first half. He explained that it
was what it was, and it was over, let's turn it around. Every Coach
I have had since I first started playing football has taught me
about the "next play" mentality. Great football players don't let
bad plays ruin future plays. If something goes wrong, shake it off,
forget about it, and reset—we can worry about it after the game.
This message still applies at the Division I level. Lea remarked
on a few problems and how we can fix them, answered a few
questions, and just like that, we were running back out the tunnel. Halftime in the locker room always flies by.

JOHN: Obviously, we needed to take care of the ball better, but
we'd done a lot of good things in the first half. Ian and Ben had
been tremendous, and I thought our defense got us out of some
tough spots. The key at that point was to not let them back into it.

The second half began, and though the defense did not come out as hot as they would have liked, they finished off the drive right. The Eagles plowed their way through the Irish to the 9-yard line. A pass break-up by Nick McCloud led to a fourth-and-1. Hafley, who probably realized that being behind by 12 isn't a whole lot better than being behind by 15, decided to keep his offense on the field. The Eagles aligned in the shotgun and handed off to running back Travis Levy, who was stopped dead in his tracks by a host of Irish defenders. Their lead intact, the Notre Dame offense took over deep in their own territory.

Their backs were against the wall, but a pair of impressive runs by C'Bo Flemister brought the Irish out to the 34-yard line. Then Book threw to Skowronek for 27, but he was stripped—the third fumble that the Irish had lost that day—and Boston College took over on their own 39. As had been the case earlier in the game, however, the Eagles gave the ball back to the Irish in short order. The following play, Irish linebacker Jack Kiser intercepted his former teammate's pass.

> **REED:** Jack was spying the QB right behind the defensive line. He started to backpedal when Jurkovec wound up. He jumped up and reeled in the pass. Jack was a very successful triple-option quarterback in high school. Indiana's Mr. Football 2018 was incredibly productive on the offensive side of the ball, passing for 59 touchdowns and rushing for 139 in his high school career. For this reason, we gave him a fair amount of smack for his pitiful two-yard interception return and poor ball security as he almost gave the ball right back to the Eagles. We knew he was better than that.

Kiser's interception provided the offense with excellent field position. C'Bo Flemister took the ball to the 1-yard line on a hard-fought 27-yard gain. On the following play, offensive coordinator Tommy Rees gave the ball right back to a deserving Flemister to run it in for six. The Eagles, unwilling to give up, respond with a 12-play, six-minute drive resulting in a touchdown by running back Dave Bailey. Irish up 38–23.

As the fourth quarter began, the Irish were once more fighting their way down the field. On a reverse sweep from the Notre Dame 43, Book handed off to Avery Davis, who used his speed to carry for a 29-yard gain. Five plays later, Book finished off the drive with an unplanned QB run for a touchdown, giving Notre Dame a commanding 22-point lead with just over 12 minutes to play in the game.

After a back-and-forth battle in the first three quarters, the Irish led by three scores and had the opportunity to effectively finish the Eagles with a stop on the ensuing drive. Boston College fair caught Doerer's kickoff and began at the 25. A four-yard gain on first down set up second-and-manageable, but Kyle Hamilton nearly intercepted a pass intended for Zay Flowers on third down to force the BC punt team onto the field. The Irish defense, tasked with stifling any attempt at an Eagles comeback, had held the Eagles to another three-and-out. On the next play, Matt Salerno returned what was just the second punt of the day for either team for a 12-yard gain to the Notre Dame 42.

JOHN: That was a critical stop for us, though I'm sure Kyle regrets not intercepting that pass on third down. He made an incredible read and might have been able to walk into the end zone had he caught it. It would have been quite the exclamation point had he managed to pull off a pick-six there, and there were a few choice words from some of the coaches on the headset when the ball bounced off his hands. All things considered, though, it was still an outstanding play.

Following the return, the offense took the field once again. Rees called a series of run plays that kept the ball within the sidelines in an attempt to run out the clock. Flemister and Tyree carried the ball to the Eagles' 30-yard line but were ultimately stopped on third down, bringing the field-goal team onto the field. Doerer lined up for the kick from 48 yards out. It had plenty of leg, but the wind forced the ball wide right, and Boston College took over with under six to play.

Behind 45–23 with five-and-a-half minutes to play, an Eagles comeback appeared rather improbable. Undeterred, however, Jurkovec led the BC offense down the field, capping off a six-play, 70-yard touchdown drive with an eight-yard touchdown throw to his tight end, Hunter Long. The Eagles completed a two-point conversion with a carry by Levy, moving the margin to 14. However, the onside kick was unsuccessful, and Notre Dame then ran out the clock with a long offensive possession. The game ended with a final score: Notre Dame Fighting Irish 45, Boston College Eagles 31.

REED: Kelly was upset with how the defense was playing, and Lea was confused by the mistakes that were made. At the end of the day, a win is a win, and we would review the team's missed assignments on Monday. I took off my headset and went to shake hands with the opposing players. A large group of Notre Dame players surrounded Phil and wished him well. Many of us were freezing, so we quickly applauded the others and ran inside.

Coach Kelly rallied the troops in the locker room after the game. This was by no means the team's best performance. Kelly explained that just because they had beat Clemson last week did not mean the season would be smooth sailing from here on out. After a week off for final exams, the Irish would be heading to Chapel Hill, North Carolina, to face their second ranked opponent of the year. The Mack Brown–coached Tar Heels had an explosive offense, led by quarterback Sam Howell and a tandem of all-conference running backs. Like Boston College, UNC was not going to go down without a fight.

CHAPTER 9

VICTORY MARCH

With the bye week over and finals in the rearview mirror, the 8–0, No. 2–ranked Irish were excited to get back to work. The narrative following the team's victory over Boston College revolved around an underwhelming performance. With Notre Dame's second ranked opponent of the year on the horizon came yet another chance for the team to prove itself.

Over the bye week, a few team members tested positive for COVID, including one of the team's strength and conditioning coaches. Fortunately, former Fighting Irish walk-on and current assistant director of football operations Tyler Plantz was there to fill the position for the week. Tyler, also known as "Tuna" by many members of the team, often frequented the Gug weight room and was well aware of Coach Balis' workout routines and schedule. As a coach who had been through the process before, many players were excited and motivated by his presence.

As the practice week progressed, players became eager to once again square off against a different-colored jersey. Fortuitously for an anxious team, this particular game was set to be played on Friday afternoon in Chapel Hill, North Carolina. Still, tensions were high on the defensive field the Wednesday before—the last padded practice before kickoff. Daelin Hayes had sacked the scout quarterback multiple times and continuously spouted discouraging remarks at the scout offense. Hayes then called out a suspiciously quiet scout-team receiver who has a knack for getting in the starting defense's head. Matt Salerno, performing his best UNC WR Dazz Newsome impersonation, buzzed past a starting corner, made an acrobatic one-handed catch, and ran for a touchdown. He then felt it necessary to share his feelings with the starting defense on his way back from the end zone. He challenged Hayes to come guard him, causing a ruckus among the players.

> **REED:** Signaling throughout practice, I got to watch a fair amount of my WOPU friends test their talents against possible NFL-bound players. Matt Salerno is by far my favorite to watch. He's an incredible athlete, and when coaches or other players failed to notice, he's not afraid to let them know. When he was a sophomore, he threatened to take a fifth-year captain's scholarship. He then toasted him one-on-one and scored a touchdown. Salerno insisted that the only way a walk-on gets noticed is if they speak up. Except he wasn't quite so eloquent in his phrasing.

Lea blew the whistle, marking the end of a long day. As the players jogged toward Coach Kelly for the final breakdown, the players mediated the situation and refocused toward the fight ahead.

The University of North Carolina Tar Heels entered the game ranked No. 19 in the country. They'd been ranked as high as No. 5 earlier in the season, and it seemed that the media believed they should have been ranked much higher. The Tar Heels held a 6–2 record to that point, with their only losses coming to Florida State and Virginia in a pair of high-scoring shootouts. With quarterback

Sam Howell in the running for the Heisman and two explosive running backs in No. 8 Michael Carter and No. 25 Javonte Williams, beating UNC would be no easy task.

Traditionally, the Irish finish the regular season over Thanksgiving weekend with a cross-country trip to California and a road date with either USC or Stanford. Though the Pac-12 had ultimately decided to go forward with a truncated six-game season, neither team was on the schedule this year—forcing Notre Dame to head southeast to the Tar Heel state. In addition, the Friday kickoff prevented the team from celebrating Thanksgiving as they normally would, with an enormous buffet at the Morris Inn.

> **JOHN:** The combination of being done with school entirely, a Friday kickoff, and the road trip to North Carolina rather than California was certainly an adjustment for some of the guys who had been around the program for a while. We certainly benefited from having had the bye week the week prior, but there's no denying that it felt different.

Following a walk-through and meetings at the Century Center downtown, the team flew to the Raleigh-Durham International Airport. After another walk-through in the hotel's parking lot the following morning, the Fighting Irish arrived at Kenan Memorial Stadium in Chapel Hill with a fire in their belly. Nick McCloud, starting cornerback and senior leader on the defense, had transferred from North Carolina State the year before. Along with his defensive skill and ability, McCloud brought intensity from the rivalry between NC State and UNC. His fervent anger and hot-blooded grimace impassioned those around him. Players fed off his energy in pregame warmups as he snarled across the 50-yard line between drills.

REED: I had no reason to resent UNC, besides the fact we were about to play them. But after seeing Nick get into a shouting match before the first whistle had even blown, I was utterly on board. The brotherhood on this team was so powerful. If anyone got into an altercation with an opposing player, every player had his back—even if that player was a grad-transfer who hadn't played a full season in the blue and gold.

JOHN: The Heels certainly weren't intimidated by us, and there was more chatter throughout the game than I would have anticipated beforehand.

Once the Tar Heels had made their way onto their sideline, the Fighting Irish stormed the field, prayed in the end zone, and assembled on the sideline. After winning the coin toss, Chris Tyree set his heels on the end zone, waiting to catch the starting kickoff. The ball sailed over his head, and Notre Dame began their drive at the 25. Book caught the first snap and searched for an open receiver downfield, to no avail. UNC forced Book out of the pocket and sacked him on the 11-yard-line. After a fruitless run by Kyren Williams, the Irish punted from deep in their own territory.

After a short-lived run by Howell, the Tar Heels decided to hand the ball off to their "more seasoned" runner. Running back Michael Carter evaded the Irish defensive line and slithered his way through the secondary before Shaun Crawford brought him down at the Notre Dame 20. Howell, unable to find an open receiver, broke out of the pocket and bustled to the 4-yard-line. On first-and-goal, the defensive backs smothered the receivers, forcing Howell to make a questionable pass to his receiver that ultimately fell incomplete. On second down, Howell handed off to Williams, who tried to run it straight up the middle. But Jayson Ademilola and Kurt Hinish filled their gaps, confusing Williams and allowing Drew White and Jeremiah Owusu-Koramoah to tackle the hesitant Williams for a loss of two. Having forced a third-and-goal, the Irish needed one more stop to force the field-goal attempt. On third down, Hayes sprinted off the edge and was a millisecond short of swatting Howell's pass before his release. Alas, the ball flew to the corner of the end zone, where cornerback Tariq Bracy leapt into the air in an attempt to break up the pass. Tar Heels receiver Emory Simmons' length, however, allowed him to reach up and over Bracy's helmet to reel in the football. The Tar Heels led 7–0.

> **REED:** The defense didn't start the way we had planned. We wanted to shut down any belief that UNC could win this game immediately. The quick three-and-out by the offense didn't leave much room for error when the possessions changed. We needed to turn the momentum of this game around fast.

> **JOHN:** Howell put the ball in the one spot where his guy could make a play on it, and they deserve a ton of credit for striking first on that drive. With that being said, players and coaches alike were upset with our performance early in the game.

After a touchback on the ensuing kickoff, a handful of passes and rushes brought the Irish close to midfield. On a second-and-6 from their own 43, Book dropped back to pass and found Mayer on a crossing route. Mayer's crafty route-running led to a 16-yard gain. From there, offensive coordinator Tommy Rees gave Chris Tyree a turn. He flaunted his speed as his piston legs rushed for 16 more. The next snap, Tyree picked up the blitzing linebacker, allowing Book to cut inside and up the field. Mid-run, he signaled Javon McKinley to block for him, allowing him to dodge defenders and utilize his teammates' blocks to get to the 7-yard-line. Kyren Williams capped off the drive with a touchdown rush up the middle.

> **REED:** This was the boost we needed. The offense steamrolled down the field—75 yards in nine plays. The UNC defense was not going to stop our offense. We just needed to stop theirs.

On the first play of the next possession, however, Howell threw to wide receiver Dazz Newsome on an orbit route behind the line of scrimmage. Newsome, known to generate yards after the catch, stopped short, causing Drew White to fly past and creating space for him to sprint along the sideline before being dragged down by Owusu-Koramoah. On the Irish 47, the Tar Heels received a holding penalty, causing second-and-15. However, UNC head coach Mack Brown had no intention of allowing the minor setback to halt their momentum. Soon thereafter, Howell heaved the ball down the field and found Dyami Brown on a deep post route. Brown, just out of the reach of Bracy, caught the ball in stride for a gain of 51 yards. Capitalizing on the big play, Howell ran the ball into the end zone from one yard out. Once again, the Tar Heels were up by seven.

> **REED:** It wasn't that we were in the wrong formations or calling bad plays—the guys weren't playing as themselves. Our corners weren't finishing through hands, our linebackers weren't running through tackles, and our defensive line was letting the ball get outside the pocket. We were out of it. But luckily, the offense was not.

The offense took the field with swagger and bravado. The first play of the drive, Book sidestepped a UNC defender and spotted Javon McKinley. He quickly chucked the ball downfield, with confidence that McKinley would be able to overpower any corner. McKinley leapt into the air as the ball landed perfectly in his hands for a gain of 43. Seconds later, Book tucked the ball into his arm and began to run. Behind the pummeling blocks of Rob Hainsey, Aaron Banks, and Tommy Tremble, he dashed toward the end zone. After shedding one tackler and stiff-arming another, Book was forced out of bounds at the 6-yard line. On second-and-goal from the 4, Book dropped back to pass. With no one open, he was chased all the way back to the 25-yard line. Finally, however, he found Kyren Williams, who caught the ball on the 10 and bulldozed through the UNC linebacker to reach paydirt. In all actuality, the "four-yard" touchdown pass involved a 15-yard throw and a 10-yard run. The game was tied 14–14.

REED: Sometimes Coach Lea would give me information to pass along to the players while the offense was playing or Coach O'Leary was busy. Other times he would ask me to put the headsets on their heads. It was awkward for me to stand there with the headset box strapped to my waistband as one of the players listened to Coach Lea. It was helpful to the players, considering it was hard to hear Lea through the old-fashioned landline telephones set up on the tables near the equipment boxes. Before the next defensive drive, Lea asked to speak with Drew White. With the headset on, Drew listened intently, nodded, and instilled faith in Coach Lea the defense was ready to play. Silently, I acknowledged the meaning and importance of this conversation, eager to see how the following drive would play out. I put the headset back on, now oozing sweat from

Drew's hair. I wrinkled my nose to get over my disgust, a small price to pay for the team's success. It was a gritty job, but someone had to do it, I reminded myself as I watched my teammates wipe blood and dirt off their faces after a tackle.

On the first play of the Tar Heels' next drive, Javonte Williams ran 10 yards, immediately earning another set of downs. The next three plays, however, were much less successful for the Tar Heels. On first down, Ade Ogundeji sacked Howell with the help of Marist Liufau and Myron Tagovailoa-Amosa. The second quarter began, but the Irish defense maintained their dominant mindset. Williams was held to a gain of three on second down, and on third-and-8, Hamilton and McCloud denied Howell's pass attempt. Just like that, the drive was over and the UNC punt team took the field.

JOHN: Obviously, it took us a little while to settle in on defense, so that stop was incredibly important for us as we attempted to slow down their attack. They came in with an excellent game plan, and they had weapons all over the field that proved very difficult to deal with. Sometimes, after a couple rough drives to start a game, you have to buckle down and prove to yourself as a unit that success is still possible—and we did that there.

UNC's punt landed on the Notre Dame 16, putting the Irish offense on a long field. Despite earning a pair of first downs, Williams was stopped short on third down at the 46, forcing the Irish to punt the ball away. Bramblett's punt was downed at the 3, flipping the field entirely. With 11 minutes left in the half, the Irish defense lined up against UNC with hopes of repeating the last drive and making quick work of Sam Howell and his posse.

Williams was held to a one-yard gain on first down, bringing the ball to the 4-yard line. On second, Owusu-Koramoah beat a block and screamed off the edge with his hands held high. Howell tucked the ball to avoid him but was instantly wrapped up by sophomore Isaiah Foskey. While being held tight, Howell scrambled forward to avoid the safety. Howell completed a pass to Williams on third down, but he was stopped short of the first-down marker. The tackle marked two consecutive drives with UNC gaining 12 yards or fewer.

> **REED:** The defense had hit its stride and found its edge. Marist had few great tackles, sparking confidence in himself. Wu's lightning speed was finally on display. Our secondary was all over the deep threats like white on rice. Everything was coming together, but there was still a lot of ball to be played.

After a hard-fought set of downs, the Irish offense again punted the ball. After another outstanding Bramblett punt, the Tar Heels once more began their drive from their 3-yard line—this time with a vengeance. Dazz Newsome caught Howell's pass and escaped for a 14-yard gain. Two plays later, Liufau blitzed the A-gap, charged the pass-blocking running back head-on, and plowed through to the quarterback. He sacked Howell on the 8 in a phenomenal display of force, setting up third-and-18. A completion to Newsome moved the chains, however, giving the Heels first-and-10 from their own 29. Several plays later, UNC once again found themselves facing another third-and-long. Howell snapped the ball and threw to an open Josh Downs well behind the chains. As Downs turned his head, Hamilton ripped toward him and lowered his head. Hamilton struck Downs and propelled him backward to the ground. Downs popped up immediately and ran toward the sideline, but the refs suspected foul play. After a review, they called Hamilton for targeting, resulting in his ejection as well as an automatic first down and 15-yard gain for UNC.

> **REED:** I know Kyle Hamilton did not mean to target Downs. Downs is a shorter player, and Kyle is very tall. Kyle tried to lower his shoulder and strike him in the hips, but because of Kyle's length and Downs' height, their helmets clashed. Losing Kyle would damage the defense for the rest of this game. Kyle is not only a skilled safety but a leader who glues our defense together.

> **JOHN:** I'm not sure what Kyle was supposed to do in that situation to avoid a penalty. He didn't lead with his head, but had to lower himself toward the ground to make the tackle. I understand the intent of the rule, but it's not fair to punish a guy simply for being 6'4" and powerful.

UNC marched down the field following Hamilton's targeting penalty, but Drew White and Kurt Hinish ultimately forced the Tar Heels into a fourth-and-2 in Irish territory. Their field-goal attempt was good from 42 yards out, and the Irish offense retook the ball. With a little over a minute left in half, Book steamed downfield. Several passes to McKinley, Skowronek, and Williams brought the Irish within field-goal range. The clock struck zero as Doerer's 32-yard kick flew through the uprights. Both teams headed back to the drawing board with a score of 17–17 at the half.

> **JOHN:** Due to space constraints, the defensive backs were forced to locker in the lacrosse locker room across the hall. Since Kyle had been thrown out of the game, it was a pretty tense

atmosphere in there. Taking on the UNC offense is challenging enough as it is, but doing so without your All-America safety is a particularly tall order. I frankly could have envisioned things going any number of different ways, but Coach Joseph did an excellent job of getting the guys settled down. He reminded us of the game plan and assured us of our ability to compete in the second half. By the time we had to return to the field, guys had calmed down and their focus was singular.

The hectic halftime scramble commenced as the coaches rallied their position groups, going over every minute detail that would give them an edge over the Tar Heels. Coach Lea cleared up a few calls and ensured the linebackers that they were doing everything correctly, with precision and force. It was troubling that it took two drives for the defense to find themselves, but now they had and needed to keep it going for another half.

REED: Every drive but our first had been an exact copy of UNC's. They would score a touchdown; we would score a touchdown. They would punt; we would punt. They would kick a field goal; we would kick a field goal. The trend had kept us in this game, but now it was time to break the pattern in our favor. The defense was ready to shut down UNC, and the offense was ready to rack up some points.

Unlike the first half, the Irish defense started fast. With an assertive blitz and tackle by Drew White for a loss of three, they held UNC to four plays and 11 yards gained. After a 62-yard punt by the Tar Heels that forced the Irish to start from their own 3, Book and the offense went straight to work. A toe-dragging reception by McKinley brought Notre Dame out to the 15. The next set of downs, Avery Davis caught a pass one yard short of the down marker. Kelly kept the offense on the field, a seemingly risky move on fourth down on their own 24-yard line. However, Book's abrupt hard count tricked UNC's defensive end to heave forward. The offside penalty awarded Notre Dame a five-yard gain and a new set of downs.

> **REED:** I've seen this done many times in practice and assumed we were trying to draw them offside. If it didn't work, we would call a timeout or take the delay-of-game penalty and punt the ball. Once again, I flipped over to the offensive channel to confirm my assumption. I heard Kelly verify that if it didn't work, we would punt. Honestly, I was surprised UNC fell for the trick. Many teams have used this strategy on fourth-and-short before. Being wary of jumping offside in this situation had become a basic protocol for defensive-line coaches.

From there, a pair of long passes to Skowronek and Mayer carried Notre Dame into the red zone. On first down, Joe Wilkins brought the Irish in range for Tommy Rees to test a new play he had conjured up that week during practice. From 13 yards out, Book snapped the ball and promptly handed it off to Skowronek, who dived in behind the offensive line. With three tight ends—Brock Wright, Tommy Tremble, and Michael Mayer—lead-blocking, Skowronek waltzed into the end zone for six. For the first time in the game, the Irish were up by seven.

> **JOHN:** Ben's a tall guy with a pretty long stride, so he's probably not who you would expect would be getting the ball on a jet

sweep. I'm sure Coach Rees knew that, so it was a great call—and it worked to perfection.

With its first lead of the game, the Irish defense dominated the second half. Every play, Howell was rushed by the defensive line and linebackers and given no open options by the secondary. On the five remaining UNC offensive drives, the Tar Heels gained a total of 47 yards: 5, 22, 7, 9, and 4, respectively. Jeremiah Owusu-Koramoah finished with nine tackles, five of which were solo. Drew White finished with five tackles, three solo, two for loss, and one sack. Although it took time for the defense to rev their engines, they operated flawlessly every play thereafter.

With under six minutes left in the fourth quarter, Notre Dame began its final drive from its own 11. Kyren Williams charged the open gap and exposed the UNC secondary. After barreling halfway downfield, Williams stiff-armed the safety until he was unable to stay in bounds. Terrific blocks by Tommy Tremble and Liam Eichenberg were paramount to the 47-yard gain. A pass to McKinley and a few more runs by Williams brought the Irish to the 14-yard line.

REED: Coach Lea was unaware of this, but sometimes when I was comfortable with our lead and didn't think Lea would need me or the headset, I would switch to the offensive channel, stand next to Matt Salerno, and repeat the play call to him. He would then tell me what the play meant and where Book's first look would be. After I recited Rees' call for this next play, Salerno smiled, shook my shoulders, and told me the pass was going to George Takacs, a close friend of ours and backup tight end. Everyone watched Takacs as he lined up. On the snap, he ran wide and caught the pass. Takacs received a fair amount of backlash for his next decision. He dove for the pylon from five yards out and landed one yard short. As George jogged to the sideline, some poked fun at him for his little dive, but all were happy for him after his catch and first down.

After the pass to George Takacs, Kyren Williams capped off his impressive performance with a one-yard touchdown rush. Notre Dame fans were not the only ones to notice Williams's success. After seeing Williams's LeBron James touchdown celebration, LeBron himself tweeted at Williams, saying, "ND Kyren Williams I see you hit em with 'The Silencer' to close out this game!"

The Irish defense smashed any hope of a UNC comeback to end the game. Ade Ogundeji sacked Howell for a loss of five, and the Irish limited UNC to two insignificant plays. UNC turned the ball over with an incomplete pass on fourth down. Book knelt twice in victory formation, and Notre Dame beat UNC in a 31–17 second-half shutout.

After the game, the locker room was jubilant. It had been a dominant second-half performance. The defense had completely shut out one of the country's most explosive offenses, and the offense had taken control of the game on the way to a two-touchdown victory. Though there were two games left to be played, the Irish appeared to be well on their way to the 23rd undefeated regular season in program history. Amid the celebration, however, Coach Kelly informed the team of some tragic news. Many of the players had already heard, but Zac Plantz—a Notre Dame alumnus and brother of Tyler and former walk-on Logan—had passed away in an automobile accident in Florida the evening prior. As Kelly implored the team to keep the family in their prayers, a pall was cast over the entire group. The overwhelming majority of individuals in the room had interacted closely with the Plantz family at one time or another during their time on campus, so this news hit the team hard.

> **JOHN:** It's impossible to overstate the impact that the Plantz family has had on an entire generation of Notre Dame football players. They're some of the kindest, most generous people you could ever meet, so it was almost incomprehensible that something like this could happen. I didn't realize it at the time, but Coach Rees paid tribute to the family, known for their love of power football, on our final touchdown. To effectively seal the game, he sent "14 personnel"—one running back and four tight ends—onto the field. Kyren scored on a one-yard run, clinching the game and immortalizing ZP in the annals of Notre Dame football history.

In an unconventional move, Kelly awarded the game ball to two separate individuals—one to Drew White, who had recorded two tackles for loss, and one to the Plantz family, in Zac's memory.

Once the story went public, the story of Zac's life spread throughout the Notre Dame community. At the time of his passing, he was actively raising money for men's health by growing a mustache in honor of "Movember." His goal was to raise $2,000, and he hadn't quite reached it on November 26. In the days and months that followed, however, those that had been inspired by Zac's story took it upon themselves to donate in his memory. When the final figures were tallied, he'd raised nearly $150,000—a testament to his charismatic personality, remarkable character, and caring spirit.

Empowered by their victory but grounded by the recent news, the Irish returned to South Bend. Kelly often emphasized the importance of "playing your best in November," and his team had clearly done that—following up their victory over Clemson with road wins over Boston College and North Carolina. However, their work was far from over and a fateful month of December still awaited them.

CHAPTER 10

....

THE BEGINNING OF THE END

Following the victory over the Tar Heels, the Irish returned to South Bend. The Friday game gave them an extra day off, which provided them the opportunity to rest, watch football, and enjoy a lavish Thanksgiving meal. The following Saturday, they'd welcome the lowly Syracuse Orange for their final home game of the season—Senior Day for the members of the class of 2021. Since the students weren't on campus, attendance would be restricted to faculty and staff, and the traditional Senior Day festivities would thus be limited. Nevertheless, the senior class was eager to close out their time in Notre Dame Stadium with a victory.

> **JOHN:** Though it was unfortunate that our parents couldn't be on the field with us before the game, I thought that the social media and communications staff did an incredible job of making us all feel honored as we prepared to play our last game at home.

However, though the Orange entered the game 1–9, film study made clear that this was a better team than their record indicated. They were well-coached, had lost a number of close games, and were just two years removed from a 10–3 season where they finished in the top 15 in both the AP and Coaches' polls. They had the talent to test the Irish, and the intense week of preparation reflected that. Additionally, the weather was another unknown—though forecasts looked decent, this would be the first home game Notre Dame had played in December since 1953. South Bend winters are notoriously unpredictable, adding another element to the team's preparation.

Since school was no longer in session, however, the schedule became more forgiving for the players. There were few early mornings, and the team's practices finished in the early evening, providing the guys with more free time than they'd had during the season. Though there wasn't a whole lot going on around town at that point, it allowed them to strengthen their already strong bonds with one another. Whether it was brunch at the Morris Inn, or card games among teammates at night, it was a unique experience for a group of individuals used to hectic schedules.

> **JOHN:** I had expected it to be really boring, so I was surprised by how much I enjoyed the time on campus with just my teammates. They gave us access to basketball tickets when the team played at home, which was fun, but I also appreciated having the opportunity to relax and "smell the roses" a little bit.

The week of practice went on largely without incident, though Thursday of game week brought some significant news about a Notre Dame football legend. On December 3, 2020, former Irish head coach Lou Holtz was awarded the United States' highest civilian award—the Presidential Medal of Freedom. At the award ceremony, President Trump remarked on the humble beginnings and extraordinary achievements of the famed Notre Dame football coach.

Holtz grew up in a small steel town in West Virginia. After serving in the ROTC program at Kent State University, he became an officer in the U.S. Army. During his coaching career, he helped six universities turn their football programs around and is, to this day, the only coach in NCAA history to bring six different football programs to a bowl game. In 2008, he was inducted into the College Football Hall of Fame. He has written three books. He has numerous philanthropic endeavors in educational opportunities, helping diabetic children, and supporting cancer research. Holtz has also visited American soldiers in 13 different countries.

Coach Holtz had a record of 100 wins, 30 losses, and 2 ties during his 11 seasons at Notre Dame. In 1988, he led Notre Dame to its 11th national championship.

In his Medal of Freedom speech, Holtz jokingly said, "When I went to Notre Dame, they had a policy. The head football coach was not allowed to make more than the president of Notre Dame. And the president of Notre Dame was a priest who took a vow of poverty. I made $95,000."

REED & JOHN: Lou Holtz knew how special this school was, speaking routinely about "the Spirit of Notre Dame." He revitalized Notre Dame's incredible tradition of excellence and set an incredible example for all who followed in his footsteps. Lou Holtz is an amazing man, father, and husband, who embodies everything that Notre Dame stands for, and we thank him for everything he has done for our university.

The team stayed healthy through the week, and following the Friday walk-through, headed downtown for meetings and dinner at the Century Center. As they went through their final paces of preparation for the last home game of the season, the team split into their offensive and defensive unit groups. In the defensive meeting, Coach Lea ran through 15 different plays on film. Every player sat in front of their own table, with each table 10–15 feet away from the next. A dispersed lattice of defensive players filled the enormous room. As the home-game traveling signaler, Reed stood at the front of the room, signaling the predesignated call that Coach Lea would use in a situation similar to the one on film. The signaler at the front of the room is part of the test. Lea wanted to ensure the players knew all the relevant signals for the week so that he could confidently use them during the game. The second part of the test was calling out individual players and quizzing them on their assignments for this call and in the situation portrayed on screen. For example, "Bo Bauer, what's your fit here?" or "Kyle Hamilton, what coverage are we in?" or "40 Dawg [Drew White], what's the check here?" Lea would ask around five to six questions to individual players per play.

> **JOHN:** Coach Lea had, honestly, an uncanny ability to catch guys who either weren't paying as much attention as they should have been or hadn't prepared enough during the week to know their specific responsibilities. It was an extremely valuable exercise for the guys.

The players took these meetings very seriously. A wrong answer could factor into the amount of playing time earned in the next day's game. The linebackers spent countless hours going over assignments, schemes, and checks in the meeting rooms after practices. Nick Lezynski was many players' go-to guy for unjudged questions and concerns. He worked tirelessly to ensure his players knew the ins and outs of Coach Lea's defense. And the work paid off.

> **REED:** The linebacker group's knowledge of the defense was unrivaled by any other position group. Yes, I have a relatively

strong bias being a linebacker myself, but it's true. The linebackers, commonly considered quarterbacks of the defense, were responsible for knowing what everyone was doing in front of them and behind them. The linebackers are the mortar that held our defensive brick wall together. And this specific linebacker group was particularly impressive. Every linebacker from top to bottom could be dropped into the defense and know their assignment. This formidable group's knowledge and awareness can largely be attributed to Nick Lezynski's extensive interpersonal skills, approachability, admirable senior leadership, and an ambitious and remarkably mature group of young guns.

As the meeting continued, players correctly answered the questions, and the coaches and players felt increasingly more confident in their preparation. After the final play on film, Coach Lea turned to face the defensive unit. He wanted to talk about incredible amounts of lies and inaccuracies in college football media. Last week, they had defeated UNC 31–17—with a stunning second-half shutout. Lea explained that he received praise from many friends and reporters for his so-called "halftime adjustments." As described previously, the team was tied 17–17 at the half and then proceeded not to let up another point in the second half. Lea reaffirmed what the team already knew—that they really didn't make any halftime adjustments. In the second half, they just started playing like themselves. They'd started slow, were overthinking, and weren't playing with their characteristic confidence. Lea changed no schemes or game plans at halftime, the team just took a step back, relaxed, and went out in the second half and played free. But that's not what the media wrote.

Alex Kirshner, cohost of the college football podcast *Split Zone Duo*, tweeted after the win over North Carolina: "Clark

Lea should probably win the Broyles Award based on the adjustments Notre Dame made after the first quarter today, whatever they were. UNC instantly morphed from elite to the worst offense in the country."

Tweets like this were what he was referring to. He wanted the team to be confident in their ability and not let the media narrative affect them, since the media clearly often doesn't know what is actually going on. He then pulled up the tape from their 2018 matchup against Syracuse at Yankee Stadium and reminded them that that game was reported as complete defensive domination. The final score was 36–3 Notre Dame. With a meaningless field goal in the last 10 seconds, Syracuse just barely escaped a shutout, and all reviews of the game labeled Notre Dame's performance as a defensive masterpiece. As he ran through the defensive drives, it became clear that the defense struggled many times throughout the game. If it hadn't been for a few big plays—namely, three interceptions, one by Jalen Elliott and two by Alohi Gilman— things could have been very different. Those three plays aside, the defense appeared to have struggled. Coach Lea used this second misinterpretation by the media to help the players understand the importance of two aspects of the game—playing with confidence and making big plays. "When we play freely," he said, "uninfluenced by others' words, we play our best. When we make big plays, we can alter the direction of the game." The message was simple but powerful, leaving the defense with a fair amount to chew on as they returned to their rooms for the night.

JOHN: After spending some time on "the inside," you learn that perception is often not reality. Though those in the media do the best they can with the information they have, it often paints an imperfect picture of what actually goes on.

Given the circumstances, Syracuse was a special game for many people on this specific Notre Dame team. However, the staff was aware that this Senior Day would be different than the class of 2021 had anticipated. Most students had already gone home, so they wouldn't be pelting each other with marshmallows inside the stadium—as is tradition. The 7,000 or so faculty, university employees, and players' guests expected to attend promised to be a less-than-raucous audience, causing many to anticipate a sterile atmosphere the following day. With this in mind, Lea wanted to make the game as memorable as possible for those who might be suiting up on these hallowed grounds for the last time. After his pep talk, he opened up the floor to the players.

Many teams lack voice and leadership—this was not one of those teams. Seniors spoke of the incredible brotherhood that existed here. Underclassmen offered their thanks to the seniors for showing them the way. Each was touching in its own way, but a few individual speeches stuck out.

Daelin Hayes reflected on his 4–8 freshman year team. He pointed out that the strong bonds that existed now were not so prevalent before. He was honored to see the sacrifices the team had to make to get to this point. Whether through winter work-outs before the sun was up or sprinting across the field with the summer sun at its highest, the mental, physical, and emotional bonds that were formed had made this team extremely special. Daelin was one of the seniors who coined "brotherhood" as one of the team's words for the season. In fact, many times, they would break their defensive huddles on "FTB," meaning "for the brotherhood." In many ways, the brotherhood mentality made the team better. The close relationships empowered others and created a sense of security. The defensive line had faith in the linebackers to back them up, and the linebackers trusted the defensive backs to cover theirs. "FTB" was not just a group of initials shouted before games, but a way of strengthening the connection among teammates and reinforcing the trust they had in one another. This bond allowed the players to feel comfortable and play freely.

Nick McCloud, who had graduate-transferred from North Carolina State before the season, spoke up after Daelin. He talked about the differences in relationships between his former team at NC State and this specific team. When Nick first joined the team, he remarked on the overwhelming feelings of welcomeness. He saw how the friendships created better people both on and off the field.

> **REED:** From my first day as a Notre Dame football player, I could tell this was a special program. When I first walked into the Guglielmino Athletics Complex (the Gug) I was greeted by four seniors, all sincere and genuine in their introductions. Later that night a few others reached out to me through Instagram, comforting me and welcoming me to the team. From firsthand experience I can say with confidence that the players recruited to Notre Dame are not only exceptional athletes, but men of character and respect. I knew McCloud's words to be true. Nevertheless, it was nice to hear it from someone who had spent four years at another Division I program.

Defensive analyst Nick Lezynski was one of the last to speak. He'd coached at Lafayette, Holy Cross, and UConn, and had walked on at Notre Dame from 2008 to 2011, so he had seen his fair share of football teams. First, he reiterated McCloud's point— his teams were not nearly as close of a group as this one. He then spoke of the respect he had for every player in the room. He was amazed by the individual effort of every player. "Everyone here has given 100 percent from the start of the season, and it has been an honor to work with you guys." A true testament to the work ethic and dedication of this team.

Many others said their piece throughout the meeting. Some players got emotional. Others became more motivated by the sentimental nature of the upcoming game. Yet again, Coach Lea was successful in his goal. He created an atmosphere for his players to speak freely and reflect on our communal journey through this crazy season. In one of the largest rooms in South Bend, they could not have felt closer to one another.

After a good night's rest in the DoubleTree, it was officially game day. The Irish took the field surrounded by the cheers of family and faculty in the stands. The emotional rush that was Senior Day drowned out the chilly December breeze. After a 12-play, 73-yard drive keyed by a 29-yard Ben Skowronek reception, Jonathan Doerer kicked in the first three points of the game from 25 yards out. However, those would be the only points of the first quarter, as both defenses forced the opponent to trade punts twice.

At the start of the second quarter, however, Syracuse came out strong. After converting three third downs, Syracuse quarterback Rex Culpepper (no relation to Daunte) connected with wide receiver Anthony Queeley for an 18-yard touchdown. Currently losing to 7–3 to an unranked team, the Irish knew they had to turn the game around. Though it took them a while, they battled through a turnover on downs to turn the tide in their favor. After the defense forced a three-and-out, Book dove into the end zone after a theatrical 28-yard run. The Irish were up 10–7.

Ahead once again, Lea wanted to be more aggressive defensively. On second-and-8 from the Orange 37, he called a blitz play that would send Owusu-Koramoah through their offensive line.

Reed signaled in the call, and "Wu" blitzed through the B gap. Culpepper narrowly escaped his grasp but was immediately forced into the arms of Drew White and Myron Tagovailoa-Amosa, who ripped the ball from his hands. Marist Liufau scooped up the forced fumble and carried it another 12 yards before being dragged down—putting on a clinic in defensive teamwork in just one play. On the next play, Book passed the ball to Javon McKinley for a 21-yard touchdown. Another Syracuse three-and-out gave possession back to the Irish, and Book connected with McKinley again for a 28-yard touchdown. Just like that, Notre Dame led 24–7 with a few seconds to play before halftime.

> **JOHN:** Clearly, we'd made some mistakes early on that kept it closer than any of us felt like it should have been, so it felt good to assert ourselves late in the half. It was an emotional day after a big win, so a sluggish start wasn't entirely unpredictable. With that being said, we held ourselves to a higher standard and knew we needed to perform better in the second half.

The Irish swaggered back onto the field after an emphatic half-time speech from Coach Kelly. After an Owusu-Koramoah forced fumble gave us the ball in Syracuse territory, we were unable to capitalize—fumbling on the first snap and giving the ball right back to the Orange. On the next drive, Syracuse running back Sean Tucker waltzed into the end zone from 40 yards out, cutting the margin to 10. The offense was unable to answer on the ensuing drive, turning the ball over once more—this time on an interception. The defense, eager to right the wrong, took the field on a mission. On first down, Culpepper attempted to take the ball outside, but was met head-on by Ade Ogundeji, who stripped the ball from his clutch. Owusu-Koramoah leapt onto the ball and held on tightly, securing possession. With the ball back in Book's hands, Notre Dame put together an eight-play, 53-yard scoring drive without the benefit of a pass. On third-and-3 from the Orange 17, Book smoothly ran it in for his second rushing touchdown of the day. Doerer's extra point was perfect, leaving the score at 31–14 Irish with approximately six minutes left to play in the third quarter.

The defense, slightly embarrassed to have allowed the Orange to have scored on them twice, took the field intending to send a message. After a Syracuse conversion, Daelin Hayes dropped back into coverage from his defensive end position and picked off Culpepper. Though he's a tremendous athlete, he visibly wasn't used to having the ball in his hands. Regardless, everyone cheered on the senior captain as he rumbled across the entire field for a respectable 13-yard return.

> **JOHN:** Sure, he gained 13 yards, but he may have covered 60. That's not a guy you get to see carry the ball very often, so it was fun to see him get that chance.

From there, the Notre Dame drive stalled, and a 50-yard attempt by Doerer fell wide right, keeping the margin at 17. The Irish defense forced another three-and-out, however, giving the offense the ball at its own 32. Capitalizing on the opportunity, Book floated a beautiful pass to a diving Javon McKinley for his third touchdown of the day—capping off a three-play, 68-yard drive.

With the Irish leading 38–14, Coach Kelly asked his coaches which young players they would like to see in action and which seniors they could get in the game. Some took the field and proved their worth, such as speed demon freshman running back Chris

Tyree, who ran in a 94-yard touchdown. Others struggled—the defense let up an 80-yard touchdown run, which led to some heated discussion over the headsets. Despite this small misstep, spirits were high, and the seniors were upbeat. Why specifically? Because the "Blue Group" was going in. The Blue Group was a punt-return team led particularly by senior walk-ons. The squad included Jack Henige, John Mahoney, Reed Gregory, Cam "Buk" Ekanayake, Patrick Pelini, and Xavier Lezynski, to name a few—all of whom were valued members of the football program, despite their limited playing time. Although their athletic ability might have been limited, their heart, effort, and work ethic continuously made this team better in more ways than one. The group performed admirably.

REED: It was an honor to be on the field on Senior day with my parents watching from the stands. With limited fans allowed inside the stadium, it was easy, although frowned upon, for people to move around the stadium. I told my parents and younger brother Harry to move right behind our bench, so I could signal to them when I would be going. Our plan worked, and they had an unobstructed view of me locking down Syracuse's long snapper. A truly incredible experience.

JOHN: It wasn't clear if they were going to punt or not, so I had to rush onto the field at the last minute. I made it out in time, but ultimately ended up running into my own teammate as I attempted to block my assignment. I didn't envision my football career ending with a face-plant, but I guess that's just how it works sometimes. Regardless, though, it meant a lot to have the opportunity to get out there one last time.

Following the Blue Team's appearance, the offense ran the clock out without incident—sending the seniors off with a 45–21 victory in their final game at home. In a traditional year, the seniors would take a picture with Coach Kelly before kickoff, then run to the 50-yard line to meet their parents. Due to COVID regulations, this year's senior appreciation ceremony was different. When the game clock struck zero, the players shook hands on the field and headed into the locker room. After the postgame speech and position meetings, the seniors walked back down the stairs, slapped the PLAY LIKE A CHAMPION sign, and took the field. Each senior took a photo with Coach Kelly under the goal post, then took a group photo with everyone. At long last, the seniors' parents were allowed on the field. All around, families embraced their players and rejoiced. It was a beautiful sight and a fitting end to an incredible journey.

REED: We took pictures with our families, with our position groups, and our friends. Understandably, it was an extremely well-documented occasion. It was the end of an era.

JOHN: It meant a lot to have the opportunity to commemorate the occasion with all the people who had made it possible. It's certainly an evening I'll remember forever, and I'm grateful that we could make it work, despite the circumstances.

Slowly, however, players meandered back inside to change. As much as they had wanted to hold on to this feeling, it was time for it to end. There was much more to accomplish, and they knew that there wouldn't be any more teams like Syracuse on the schedule. They knew they'd have to be at their very best in the weeks that followed to achieve all they knew they were capable of.

CHAPTER 11

THE REMATCH

Before the Irish faced Syracuse, but after they had defeated North Carolina, they clinched their spot in the ACC Championship Game in perhaps the most anticlimactic way possible. In the interest of fairness, the powers that be in the ACC decided that eligibility for the conference championship game would be based on a nine-game conference schedule, rather than the originally scheduled 10—effectively canceling the games scheduled for December 12. So, rather than head to Winston-Salem to face Wake Forest, the Irish stayed in South Bend, fully intent on using this extra time to their advantage. The objective for the week was clear—rest up, get healthy, and turn the focus completely to the rematch with Clemson, who had earned a place in the title game with a dominant second-half performance in Blacksburg against Virginia Tech. After a few days off the field, the team returned to practice on Thursday with a renewed focus on fundamentals. The scout teams had the day off, and the first teams on both sides of the ball had the chance to scrimmage one another.

> **JOHN:** Obviously, this was our first experience in conference play, so everything seemed new to us. However, it was particularly strange to come out of the showers after Monday's workout to learn that we'd be heading to Charlotte regardless of what

happened that weekend. It didn't change our approach, but I guess I had anticipated something more memorable.

Further complicating the defensive preparation were revelations, reported by *Sports Illustrated* earlier in the season, that Clemson had "mastered the (totally legal) art of sign stealing." And though there had long been rumors that this had been the case, it nevertheless forced the Irish to adjust their strategy. Mainstays of the playbook—used even in prior seasons—needed to be reimagined, forcing the defensive signalers to get creative in imagining new signals.

JOHN: Our calls are structured so that "families"—or terms that are in some way related to one another—refer to similar things. It makes sense logically, but can prove challenging when you need to come up with 12 different hand signals referring to avian wildlife, U.S. cities, or firearms. We were lucky school was out that week, because it took some time for us to redo a couple years' worth of work.

REED: There are only so many ways to represent birds using hand signals. John and I put our thinking caps on and got the creative juices flowing. We made signals that were so thought out and far-fetched that they could only be explained by following our word-association path. At this point in the season, we had created hundreds of signals that John, Pat, and I could recall and perform instantly. However, that was not necessarily the hard part. We were also assigned to teach every player the signals and guarantee they would recognize them while on the field. This week proved to be more difficult as Coach Lea wanted us to alternate between old and new signals for the same calls at our discretion. A challenging task but a load we had to bear.

As the sun rose on Monday of game week, however, some long-standing rumors began to swirl more intensely about a member of the coaching staff. That morning, national media began to report that defensive coordinator Clark Lea—a Vanderbilt alum— had been offered the head coaching position at his alma mater. As speculation continued to mount on Twitter, the Irish found themselves in something of a holding pattern. A team meeting was scheduled for 12:45, and the team eagerly anticipated an announcement one way or another. Once the meeting started, Coach Kelly approached the situation matter-of-factly, congratulating Coach Lea on this tremendous honor and informing the team that he had, in fact, accepted the position. After promising to schedule the Commodores at some point in the near future, he gave the floor to Coach Lea, who—amid cheers and congratulations from everyone in the socially distanced auditorium—expressed his gratitude for this opportunity and affirmed his commitment to the tasks that still lay ahead of this year's team.

> **REED:** Multiple times in meetings, Coach Lea would say that his goal was to become a head football coach. He presented his goal in a manner that would inspire us to create long-term goals for ourselves. As a senior on the team, I was less sad to see him leave and more happy for him and what he had accomplished. Lea was more than deserving of this opportunity.

> **JOHN:** As he announced this news, Coach Kelly made a good point—things like this are the price of success in college football.

> Everyone was sad to see Coach Lea leave, but when you have success like we'd had over the last few years, it was inevitable.

Following those three days of practice, the Irish had Saturday evening and Sunday off before beginning a standard week of game preparation, even though their game had been canceled. Saturday became something of a universal "makeup date" across college football. As the only matchup of ranked teams, UNC-Miami was the headliner—and though rivalry games like Wisconsin-Iowa and USC-UCLA were slated to occur, it wasn't expected to be a particularly impactful day, at least as far as the playoff picture was concerned. The only team playing that day that was still in the hunt was sixth-ranked Florida, whose only loss was to then–No. 5 Texas A&M. They were slated to face lowly LSU—who, following their national championship season the year before, had limped to a 3–5 record. Most observers' eyes were already on the championship games set to occur the following week: Florida-Alabama and Clemson–Notre Dame.

In such a fickle year, however, it was foolish to think that things would go according to plan. Against the odds—and with just 54 scholarship players—the "Bayou Bengals" found themselves tied, with the ball and a chance to win as the clock showed 2:51. Their first series stalled, and a third-down completion was unable to move the chains, presumably forcing a punt. However, as he made the tackle, Florida defensive back Marco Wilson removed the LSU player's shoe—and proceeded to hurl it 20 yards downfield. This earned him an unsportsmanlike-conduct penalty, extending the Tigers drive. Six plays later, LSU kicker Cade York connected on a 57-yard field-goal try, giving Kyle Trask and the Gators offense just 23 seconds to prevent a stunning upset. A last-second, 51-yard field-goal attempt by Florida sailed wide left, effectively dashing their playoff hopes. A 474-yard performance by Trask was wasted, and the playoff picture suddenly seemed clearer.

In South Bend and across the country, Irish fans reacted with a mixture of shock and relief. For the past week, the playoff speculation hadn't stopped. What if Florida beats Alabama, and Clemson beats us? What would the committee do with Ohio State, which had played just five regular-season games? Following the Gators' loss, however, it seemed that there was a good chance that Notre Dame would be in no matter what. After all, they were still undefeated, the win over Clemson was the best win in college football that year, and their road win over UNC was looking better and better every day.

> **JOHN:** There were a few of us who were watching the game together, and once we got past the hilarity of the whole shoe-throwing incident, we realized that the status quo had changed. Don't get me wrong, we knew we still needed to play well the next week, but the most likely scenario by which we would get left out of the playoff had just vanished. With that being said, it's games like that that make two undefeated regular seasons in three years that much more impressive.

As Monday rolled around, however, the focus turned exclusively to the task at hand. The Irish entirely controlled their own destiny—a win that weekend would assure them a spot in the playoff, as well as a likely No. 2 seed. However, the Clemson Tigers were at nearly full strength—Lawrence had returned, along with Skalski, Davis, and Jones Jr. They'd raced through the rest of their ACC schedule, blowing past Pittsburgh and Virginia Tech to leave them 9–1 and ranked No. 3 heading into Saturday's matchup. The oddsmakers in Vegas were bullish on the Tigers' chances, setting them as a nearly 10-point favorite.

> **REED:** I was happy to hear we would be playing the Tigers at full strength. I believe we were better than when we last faced each other. The team was well-rested, prepared, and ready for the rematch, not to mention there was now nothing the media could say to diminish a win this weekend.

In South Bend, the week of practice was remarkably normal. The team received a "gift suite" for their participation in the championship game—a pleasant surprise for a group stuck away from home during the Christmas season and accustomed to waiting for the bowl game to receive presents. Since they'd had an extra week to prepare, the load in practice was rather light, even for a late-season game. On Tuesday and Wednesday—normally the heaviest days—players were on the field for no longer than 90 minutes. Clearly, load management and freshness was a priority for Kelly and his staff during the week of preparation.

Following Friday's walk-through, the travel roster—which had been expanded to include every senior, as well as a few other players—headed to downtown South Bend, as they had all season. Following a meal and team meetings at the Century Center, they departed for the airport, ready for their second flight to North Carolina in just over three weeks. Upon their arrival, they proceeded to the Le Méridien hotel in downtown Charlotte—which was completely decked out in ACC Championship regalia. With an afternoon kickoff scheduled for the following day, the players retired to their rooms to get off their feet, watch a little more tape, and get some rest.

JOHN: I went back to my room to practice some of the calls for that week, but got distracted for a while by the panoramic view of downtown Charlotte I had from my room. There was something about it that just added to the mystique and excitement for the following day.

Following breakfast the next morning, the team again met—first together, for special teams, then in position groups. At the end of the special teams meeting, as he often did, Coach Polian shared a quote that reflected the mood of the room extraordinarily well:

> Give every bit of yourself. Hold nothing back. Life cannot deny itself to someone who gives his all.

Following lunch and some final words from Coach Kelly, the buses left for Bank of America Stadium. Though they'd missed out on opportunities to play in a few of them that season, NFL locker rooms were old hat for the Irish at this point, and the pregame routine went on as it normally did. The defense went to midfield for a prayer before returning to prepare for warmups—though some of the players had to dress in the hallway *behind* the locker room.

JOHN: I was used to not being able to dress in the actual locker room at that point, but I did have to check my ego when I tried to take the field and was stopped by a security guard—who apparently didn't believe I was a member of the team. Thankfully, Coach Joseph was there, and he was able to convince him that I was, in fact, part of the team.

REED: I was walking about 10 feet behind John when it happened. I snickered and gave him a pat on the back when we reached the field. This was not the first, nor the last time a walk-on would be mistaken for a fan.

Following pregame warmups, as the socially distanced stadium began to fill in, the Irish returned to their locker room amid cheers from the Notre Dame faithful. After a few quiet moments discussing the final pregame adjustments, the team gathered for Kelly's pregame speech, which centered around execution, traits, and the team's preparedness for what lay before them. From there, the team left the locker room and took a long walk through the foggy tunnels beneath the stadium as they prepared to take the field. As "I'm Shipping up to Boston" played over the loudspeaker, torches spit flames and the undefeated Irish took the field.

JOHN: The vibe in the tunnel was probably the coolest I've ever encountered before a game. There's nothing like the tunnel at Notre Dame Stadium, but the production value here was incredible. The fog, the music, the flames—all of it made for a really memorable experience.

REED: The field-level suites had glass in the back, facing the tunnel. Cheers and boos alternated every window as we strutted past. I tried to stay serious and focused, but I couldn't help but smile at the rowdy fans.

After both teams took the field, Ade Ogundeji went to midfield to represent Notre Dame at the opening coin toss. Clemson won, but elected to defer—meaning that the Irish would start the game with the ball. Following a rare non-touchback by Clemson kicker B.T. Potter, a Chris Tyree return brought the ball to the Notre Dame 21. The 2020 ACC Championship Game—the first in Notre Dame program history—was underway. Following carries by Kyren Williams on first and second down, a third-down completion to Michael Mayer kept the drive alive. An Avery Davis catch brought them across midfield, where—following a loss of five on first down—Book again connected with Mayer on third down to move the chains. On their first drive of the day, the Irish already found themselves in field-goal range.

Unfortunately, however, their momentum slowed from there. Another negative play on first down led to a third-down sack, leaving Notre Dame with a fourth-and-13 at the Clemson 33. With a tough choice in front of him, Kelly elected to send the field-goal team onto the field for a 51-yard field-goal attempt, which would be, if successful, the longest in the history of the ACC Championship Game. Following a perfect snap and hold, Doerer snuck the ball over the crossbar, giving the Irish an early 3–0 lead.

JOHN: It was a huge kick. From that distance, nothing is guaranteed, and to take an early lead like that was huge. He came to the sideline and told me that the ball felt flat—which makes such a long kick even more impressive.

From there, Lawrence and the Clemson offense hoped to answer. Etienne returned the Irish kickoff to the 21. The Irish defense held firm on the first two plays, forcing a third-and-9. Notre Dame brought pressure, but Lawrence found E.J. Williams over the middle for a gain of 15 to keep things moving for the Tigers. Two plays later, a face-mask penalty against the Irish brought Clemson across midfield, and it appeared as if the Tigers offense was well on its way to countering Notre Dame's first move. On second down, however, Drew White deflected a Lawrence pass over the middle. The ball careened into the hands of Kyle Hamilton, who corralled it and returned it to the Irish 38. The first big play of the day had come, and suddenly, the Irish had the ball with a lead—as well as excellent starting field position.

> **JOHN:** We'd heard it over and over again, but once more it rang true—ball disruption is absolutely critical to good defense. After Kyle made that pick, I couldn't have been more optimistic. The team was excited, and it felt like everything was breaking our way early in this one.

> **REED:** Being the closest person to the field on the sideline, I loved running out to meet the players after big plays and turnovers. The defense would huddle around whoever recovered the fumble or caught the interception and jump and yell enthusiastically. Here, Kyle ran downfield before getting mobbed by his teammates. I ran over to Drew to slap him on the helmet and celebrate his interception causing tip.

With the momentum on their side, Book and the Irish offense wasted no time—finding Ben Skowronek for a gain of 26 on first down. Soon thereafter, a 24-yard carry by Williams brought Notre Dame to the Tigers 10. In just three plays, they'd gained over 50 yards—and appeared to be on their way to extending their lead to two scores. However, two Williams carries weren't enough to reach paydirt, and a Book incompletion on third down again brought the kicking team onto the field. This time, however, a 24-yard try from Doerer bounced off the right upright, keeping the Irish advantage at three. An enormous opportunity had been squandered, and Clemson took possession with a minute-and-a-half to play in the first quarter.

Then, on the third play of the Tigers drive, Lawrence redeemed himself for his mistake on the previous drive—finding Amari Rodgers on a post route for a 67-yard score. In the blink of an eye, Clemson had taken a lead—deflating the Irish sideline that just minutes before had been ecstatic. Potter's extra point was good, and the Tigers led 7–3 as the first quarter neared a close.

> **JOHN:** I'll give credit where it is due—it was an outstanding play call and even better execution by Lawrence and Rodgers. He clearly identified single coverage before the snap, and was able to look Kyle off to create space over the middle of the field—no easy task for a guy that long and rangy. He delivered a perfect throw, and the rest is history. The margins are so small against a team like that, and they made us pay on that one.

On the ensuing drive, the Irish offense once again got off to a fast start. A first-down carry by Avery Davis was followed by a 30-yard completion to Tommy Tremble, and after just two plays, Notre Dame found itself in Clemson territory for the third time already that afternoon. However, in what was becoming a recurring theme in Charlotte that afternoon, they were unable to finish the drive. Three carries by Williams left Kelly in a tough spot—try another field goal, this time from 45 yards out, or go for it on fourth-and-3. He kept his offense on the field, but Book was unable to connect with Davis along the right sideline, forcing a turnover on downs. Leading 7–3, Lawrence and the Clemson offense took the field once again.

Starting at their own 28, the Tigers wasted little time—moving quickly into Notre Dame territory on a completion to Williams and a keeper by Lawrence. An Etienne carry on third-and-2 kept them moving, and on second-and-4, Lawrence found Williams over the middle. Williams rumbled into the end zone, extending the Tigers' lead even further. Another Potter extra point made it 14–3, and the Irish suddenly found themselves behind the proverbial eight-ball.

> **JOHN:** Suddenly, it felt like things were getting away from us. We'd started off so well, but couldn't finish drives—which is something you absolutely have to do against teams as explosive and talented as Clemson.

Following a Potter touchback, Book provided a glimmer of hope for the Irish faithful, finding Mayer for a gain of nine on first down. However, two consecutive sacks forced an Irish punt, which Bramblett booted 51 yards to the Clemson 27. From there, the Clemson offense continued their assault, recording gains of 15, 11, 24, and 11 on their first four plays—earning their way to the Notre Dame 12. However, the Irish defense stiffened, and a third-down pass breakup by freshman cornerback Clarence Lewis brought the Clemson kicking team onto the field. Potter connected from 27 to extend the Tigers lead to 14, but Notre Dame could feel good about keeping them out of the end zone.

> **REED:** Freshman cornerback Clarence Lewis, also known as "T-Bone," played a prominent role in our defense. From the first week of camp, Lewis proved he was a playmaker and wouldn't be long for the sideline. He earned his starting spot and proved he belonged every game. This was an imperative stop on third-and-8 and scored four points in our RBI defense. Stopping the Clemson Tigers on the 10-yard line was pivotal to the defense's success.

Unfortunately, despite another promising start on first down, the Irish were unable to counter the Tigers' score. Forced to punt yet again with just over two minutes remaining in the half, it was absolutely imperative that they stop the bleeding and prevent Clemson from taking a three-score lead before halftime. On fourth down, Bramblett continued his strong performance, booting a 47-yard punt that was fair caught on the Clemson 12.

All things considered, the drive began relatively well for the Notre Dame defense. Following a false-start penalty and an incomplete pass, Etienne carried for eight yards, leaving the Tigers with third-and-7, deep in their own territory. They bled the clock, calling a timeout with just 1:19 to play. Many fans likely thought they were done for the half. However, a third-down draw by Etienne—keyed, believe it or not, by a Lawrence block—gained 15 yards to keep the Tigers offense in business. Another first down—and quick spike by Lawrence—left them at their own 47 with 42 seconds to play. A quick completed pass brought them into Notre Dame territory, where they spiked the ball again, leaving them with fourth-and-1 from the Irish 44. The Irish substituted for what they anticipated would be a short-yardage play, but they were unable to tackle Etienne—who went around the left end for a 44-yard score, capping a 10-play drive that ultimately left the Irish behind 24–3 just seconds before halftime.

JOHN: Their decision to spike the ball on third down surprised me—I figured they would run a quick play to attempt to get the first down, then stop the clock and assess their options. Since it was a hurry-up situation, we didn't have our short-yardage personnel on the field, and there was a brief moment of confusion on the headset as the coaches debated what to do next, while we tried to get the guys out there in the correct spots.

We ultimately got the call in, but they made a great play call and found a weak spot in our defense. You can't give a player as good as Etienne space like that, and he made us pay for it. It was a gut punch at the end of what had already been a pretty disastrous half defensively.

Following a fair catch by Chris Tyree, Notre Dame took a knee and limped into halftime, shell-shocked and in need of inspiration. The second quarter had been an unmitigated disaster, and the tone in the locker room was somber—a far cry from the excitement and anticipation that coursed through everyone before the game. As the coaches made their adjustments, the team attempted to come to grips with what had happened—and how it could be fixed moving forward. Before the team returned to the field, Coach Kelly got up and addressed the team, emphasizing the importance of execution, following the game plan, and saying frankly that "our playoff hopes depend on our performance in this second half." Frustrated yet eager for another opportunity, the Irish returned to the field.

JOHN: When Coach Kelly said that, he certainly got everyone's attention. In some sense, he was just saying the quiet part out loud, but he undoubtedly made very clear what we were playing for in that second half. It wasn't so much that we didn't think we could win the game at that point—to a man, everyone in that locker room truly believed we could—but the situation, given all that had happened in the first half, was now more complicated than that. In a year with so much uncertainty, the last thing anyone wanted to do was leave things to chance, and it was now obvious that the second half was our opportunity to make sure we put ourselves in the best position possible moving forward.

Clemson, who had won the opening coin toss and elected to defer, was slated to receive the ball at the beginning of the second half—putting the onus on the Irish defense to start the half strong and establish some momentum. Despite a 37-yard Etienne return on the kickoff, they did just that, forcing a quick three-and-out thanks to a Shaun Crawford pass breakup. If there was ever a time for the Irish offense to step up, this was it. Down three scores, they needed to show signs of life if Notre Dame was to have any chance to make a comeback.

> **REED:** Holding Lawrence to five positive yards on the first drive of the half was a powerful confidence boost. We could play with this team. A five-yard tackle for loss, followed by a Shaun Crawford pass breakup—our defense could restrain the Tigers. Now we needed the offense to come out firing.

Unfortunately, there was no pulse to be found. Three negative plays forced yet another punt, and Clemson again took over with good field position—this time near midfield. However, a holding penalty slowed them before they could really get going, and the Irish defense forced a second straight punt, which was fair caught by Salerno at the Notre Dame 12. With 9:14 to play in the third quarter, it was imperative that the Irish cut the deficit on this drive.

Despite averting absolute calamity on a Michael Mayer fumble, the offense was again unable to get anything going. This time around it did muster a first down but was nevertheless forced to punt yet again from deep within its own territory. As time continued to tick off the clock, the chances of a comeback grew even slimmer. Following a 59-yard punt by Bramblett, the Tigers took over on offense from their own 17.

Following the punt, the first two snaps for the Irish defense went as well as they could possibly have hoped. Justin Ademilola deflected Lawrence's pass on first down, and a quarterback keeper on third down went nowhere—leaving the Clemson offense with a third-and-9. In desperate need of a stop, Notre Dame showed pressure pre-snap. With limited time to throw, Lawrence released a long pass down the left sideline. At first glance, it appeared to be too long, but E.J. Williams made an acrobatic one-handed catch to gain 22 yards and extend the Tigers drive.

> **JOHN:** I was right there to see it, and as much as I wanted to believe that he hadn't completed the catch, he clearly had. It was one of the best catches I'd ever seen—the pass appeared to be over his head, but he was able to secure it with just his right hand and maintain complete control as he fell. It was excellent coverage by Clarence, too. Lawrence put it in the one place where his guy could grab it, and Williams made an incredible effort to haul it in. Coach Lea called down from the box, hoping that something had happened to jar the ball loose as he went to the ground. Coach Elston saw it as closely as I did, however, and he quickly confirmed that Williams had, in fact, caught it. We absolutely needed a stop there, so that was a crushing blow for us as we tried to get back into the game.

From there, a pair of Etienne carries brought the Tigers offense past midfield, down to the Irish 34. Then, on third-and-1, Lawrence found a hole on a designed quarterback run and ran completely untouched for another touchdown. Clemson now led 30–3—the final score of the calamity in Arlington nearly two years prior—with under four minutes to play in the third quarter.

Potter's extra point extended the lead to 28, and the already long odds for the Irish grew even longer.

> **JOHN:** I will say this—with as much attention as we paid to him as a thrower—I don't think we properly appreciated Lawrence's ability to make plays with his feet. He's so tall that it doesn't necessarily look like he's running that fast, but make no mistake—he can absolutely move. Though Uiagalelei had an incredible game in the first matchup, Lawrence's athleticism added a dimension to their offense that was very challenging to deal with.

Facing a four-touchdown deficit as they took the field, the Irish offense was once again unable to sustain any success. A Ben Skowronek catch on first down was supplemented by a personal foul against the Tigers, moving the Irish across midfield before a short Williams run and two Book incompletions brought up fourth down. A completion to Tremble was negated by a holding penalty, forcing yet another Notre Dame punt. As the end of the third quarter neared, the Irish still trailed 31–3.

Continuing their momentum from the drive before, Lawrence and the Tigers offense proceeded to construct a 12-play, 66-yard drive that ended in a 37-yard Potter field goal—and, perhaps more importantly, took more than six minutes off the clock. The Irish regained possession with 10:31 to play, and though a Chris Tyree touchdown on the following drive added a touch of respectability to the final score, it was far from enough to even make things interesting. With eight minutes to play, it was clear that the proverbial party was all but over. Punts by both teams did little to change things, and the game ended 34–10. Clemson had avenged their loss from six weeks earlier, and the Irish had fallen well short of the mark in their program's first conference championship game appearance.

After the game, the Notre Dame locker room was virtually silent. After such a disappointing performance, there was little to say. Coach Kelly's postgame speech, magnanimous and honest as it was, did little to lift the team's spirits. For the first time that season, we'd been beaten—and beaten badly. On top of that, the future suddenly seemed uncertain—though our spot in the play-off had seemed virtually unassailable that afternoon, the ground appeared to be shifting beneath us.

> **REED:** In the overflow locker room for the walk-ons, which was just the hallway behind the locker rooms, we could hear Clemson celebrating one room over. A gut-wrenching sound after approaching the game with such confidence. I believe we could and should have won that game. We never got into our rhythm, and it hurt us. The loss was a double-edged sword. It damaged our spirit and diminished our playoff chances. All we could do now was hope.

After a slow start, Ohio State had taken care of Northwestern earlier in the day, and Clemson had undeniably earned a spot with their victory that afternoon. The SEC Championship Game was scheduled for that evening, but Alabama's dominance all season left them all but assured of earning a bid—even in the unlikely event of a loss. At that point, no two-loss team had ever made the playoff—seemingly ruling out Florida and Big 12 champion Oklahoma—but one-loss Texas A&M remained. Sure, they'd been blown out by the Crimson Tide earlier in the year, but they'd played well since then in the vaunted SEC West. After capping off an 8–1 regular season with a victory over Tennessee that afternoon, head coach Jimbo Fisher took advantage of the opportunity to publicly lobby for his team. Asserting that the Aggies play in the "best league in ball," he urged the committee to include them—invoking the fact that there had never been a one-loss SEC team excluded from the playoff. And though his comments—made prior to the ACC Championship Game—were likely aimed at 6–0 Ohio State, the status quo had changed following the debacle in Charlotte. The 2018–2019 playoff wasn't that far from people's memory, and fans, pundits, and analysts across America suddenly began to question Notre Dame's worthiness for that final spot.

> **JOHN:** By every statistical measure, we deserved to get in. We had more wins over Top 25 teams, a superior average margin of victory, and—despite the loss in the rematch—still had a win over a surefire playoff team. And though I was confident that our résumé would ultimately stand up to scrutiny, the reality was that things were beyond our control at that point. When the chips are down, anything can happen, and there's an inescapable sense of anxiety that comes with that.

From the stadium, the Irish headed directly to the airport. It was a somber flight back to South Bend, and the team returned just in time to see Alabama come out victorious in a 52–46 thriller over Florida. Three spots in the four-team playoff had effectively been filled. The Notre Dame faithful, however, wouldn't learn their destiny until the following afternoon. As a cold wind blew through Northern Indiana, what had been a disastrous day for the program drew to an uneasy close. For the Fighting Irish, the fate of the 2020 season hung in the balance, and all they could do was wait.

CHAPTER 12

THE (TEXAS) ROSE BOWL

Following the loss, the Fighting Irish were given the day off—though none of them awoke feeling particularly relaxed on that Sunday morning. It had been a long flight home from Charlotte, and morale was low. As the sun rose over South Bend on December 20, 2020, the uncertainty the team had felt the night before had not subsided. That afternoon was the selection show, where the Irish would learn whether or not the prior afternoon's performance had moved them into a non-playoff game—likely the Orange Bowl. In a normal year, the team would convene to watch the show if there was a good chance of making the playoff. With COVID-19 protocols in mind, however, no such gathering occurred. This year, the team was sent a mere text notification that the selections would air at 12:15 PM on ESPN.

REED: I woke up slowly that morning and meandered over to John's house to watch the selection show with the rest of the walk-ons. The first three teams were pretty much guaranteed. Our biggest fear was that we had lost by so many points to Clemson that Texas A&M would replace us in the top four.

JOHN: That morning, I went to Mass at the basilica and, in an attempt to get my mind off what awaited us that afternoon, took a long walk around the lakes. I'd thought about it every which way and was reasonably confident that we'd ultimately get the nod, but I knew that crazier things had happened. I'm the type to overanalyze things, so it was cathartic to get away for a few minutes and make peace with whatever was to come.

Since 2014, a 13-member committee has chosen four teams to make the College Football Playoff based on their performance throughout the season. The committee evaluates the teams using various relevant criteria:

- Conference championship outcome
- Strength of schedule
- Head-to-head results
- A comparison of results against common opponents

As conference champions, Alabama and Clemson took Nos. 1 and 2 right off the bat. Regardless of Ohio State's shortened six-game season, the committee believed their wins were powerful enough to earn them the third spot. As they sought to discern which team was worthiest of the fourth and final spot, Notre Dame's résumé was compared to that of Texas A&M and Cincinnati. The 8–1 Texas A&M Aggies were a respectable team but had lost by 28 points to Alabama at the beginning of the season and hadn't played a ranked team since the second week of October. The 9–0 Cincinnati Bearcats were coming off a dominant regular season, but with a strength-of-schedule ranked 77th, their wins didn't carry much weight.

REED: Even with our 24-point loss to Clemson, we still had beat them earlier in the year and had an undefeated regular season with a 10th-ranked strength of schedule. There was very little doubt in my mind that we would make it in. A&M wouldn't knock us out of the playoff.

With more suspense than necessary, ESPN's coverage team updated their display and announced that Notre Dame was the fourth and final team chosen for the 2020 College Football Playoff.

REED: The walk-ons gave out a small cheer, followed by a confused gasp as the ESPN commentators declared that No. 1 Alabama would face No. 4 Notre Dame in the Rose Bowl at AT&T Stadium in Arlington, Texas. We looked around at each other in awe as we were reminded of the last time we set foot in Jerry World. Flashbacks to our 2018 Playoff Semifinal 30–3 loss against Clemson ran through my head, sending a chill down my spine.

JOHN: Obviously, our previous trip to Arlington had ended pretty poorly. The opponent would be different this time, but the parallels were obvious—and we knew that the Tide would present their own set of challenges. I'd assumed that if we made it in, we'd be playing in the Sugar Bowl, so it was certainly a surprise to learn that we'd be heading to Texas. At that point, it wasn't even clear if the game could even legally be called the Rose Bowl since it wasn't going to be hosted in Pasadena. As a Midwest kid, I'd grown up dreaming of playing in the Rose Bowl, so on one hand it was something of a dream come true. On the other, it just felt like we'd been cheated. I mean, just imagine that iconic Pasadena sunset shining off our gold helmets.

The matchup was set for January 1, 2021, leaving the teams over a week and a half to prepare. With Christmas approaching, Alabama head coach Nick Saban allowed his players three days off to return home to celebrate the holiday with their families. Notre Dame players were not allowed that luxury. Granted, Notre Dame players' homes cover a more significant portion of America than Alabama's players, but it was nevertheless unfortunate for a group of guys who hadn't been home in more than six months.

REED: I had missed Christmases at home due to football in the past, but this year's Christmas felt particularly gloomy. Students had left campus weeks ago, and we were forced to pass the time on our own. One day, I traveled with John and Jack Henige to a Christmas tree farm to cut down my tree and put it up in my house. Being the only person living in my home at the time, I decorated the tree with lights and various items around the house while my roommates watched on FaceTime. It sounds sad, but it was gratifying and took up a whole afternoon. Although it wasn't always easy, we became quite creative and made the best out of our situation.

JOHN: We had a beautiful white Christmas in South Bend, but I'd be lying if I said I didn't wish I was back home with my family. I understood why things were the way they were, but it was a pretty lonely feeling.

Preparation began in earnest the following Monday with meetings and a light lift. The players were able to ease into the upcoming game plan while recovering from last Saturday's game. As the week progressed, the players showed signs of an uplifting disposition and motivation. Clemson's looming gray clouds had come and gone, and the team was clear-headed and ready to get back to work. Christmas, the following Friday, helped raise everyone's spirits as well. There were no meetings on Christmas Eve, but there was Mass for the team, staff, and staff families. They sat on chairs spread around the field of the IAC, listening to Father Nate. Following the service, Coach Kelly marched on the field, arms held wide, in a full Santa costume, singing an admittedly crude version of Bruce Springsteen's "Santa Claus Is Coming to Town." He sat on a velvet chair placed to the left of the altar. First, Kelly called up the team captains to sit with him. Partially confused and embarrassed by the decision, Ade Ogundeji and Shaun Crawford refused to answer Coach Kelly's questions accurately. No smiles covered the captains' faces, but the rest of the team laughed hysterically. When the commotion ended, players scrambled to find their gifts next to Santa's chair and were free to leave. The gifts were a pair of Under Armour sneakers, a shirt, and a pair of shorts. The following gift came in the form of a recurring Brian Kelly joke. Whenever the team was given time off, Coach Kelly would announce, "You all have this afternoon off, tonight off, tomorrow morning off, tomorrow afternoon off, tomorrow night off, and the next morning off," playfully saying that they just had tomorrow off. Some found it amusing—others were visibly less enthused.

> **REED:** After practice, the linebacker group exchanged Secret Santa gifts. Some very curious and humorous presents were exchanged, including a personalized Bo Bauer sweatshirt and a humorously sculpted chocolate candy bar. I received some funny T-shirts and Hawaiian chocolates from Marist Liufau. And I'm pretty sure I surprised Wu with my gifts to him. He opened his bag to find a harmonica and red betta fish in a small plastic tank. I got laughs from the rest of the room, but Wu, however, was unamused. Thankfully, Nick Lezynski brought the fish home to his children. "Jellybean" lived a "long," happy life in the Lezynski household.

Players dispersed to their living areas, whether it was off-campus houses or with many other team members at the Morris Inn on campus. The players celebrated Christmas Eve together as the snow began to pile up in South Bend.

> **REED:** Christmas morning, I woke up to my empty house and walked downstairs. When I opened the door, over a foot of snow slid inside—a classic White Christmas in beautiful South Bend. I sat next to my Christmas tree, where I had placed the cardboard care-package my family had sent me and called my mom on FaceTime. Through my little five-by-three-inch iPhone screen, I could see that Christmas had carried on as usual back in New Jersey. I watched as my family opened up the gifts I had sent them while the dogs trampled across the wrappings. It was a wonderful sight, and it made me feel much better about my situation. After gifts were opened and well wishes said, I wiped the snow off my car and drove through the blizzard over to WOPU house to enjoy their company.

If the team wasn't allowed to go home for Christmas, having a shortened amount of time off wasn't the worst thing. There aren't many things to do in South Bend during a pandemic with no other students around. More time off would have only intensified feelings of isolation, so getting back to work was a welcome distraction.

As game week neared and the Irish game plan was finalized, the herculean charge that awaited the defense became clearer. The Crimson Tide offense had been historically prolific during their 2020 campaign. Offensive coordinator Steve Sarkisian oversaw an attack that featured three Heisman Trophy contenders and averaged nearly 50 points per game. Notre Dame was a team built on establishing and maintaining control—of the ball, of the tempo, and of the game's physicality. They knew that they couldn't keep up if the game turned into a shootout, so the coaching staff devised a strategy designed to neuter Alabama's strengths and keep their offense off the field for as long as possible. This involved, as Kelly put it, playing "defense on offense"—taking advantage of our strength on the offensive line by bleeding the play clock and avoiding negative plays. If we could do this, we thought, we could stay within striking distance into the second half, where anything could happen.

> **JOHN:** I thought it was a brilliant idea. Nobody was going to beat Alabama doing the same things that they did—we'd seen that as they romped through their conference schedule that fall. It would ask a lot of our offense, but it's hard to argue with the underlying logic.

After a series of long practices and late nights, it was finally time to make the trip back to Dallas, Texas. The team tested for COVID early Wednesday morning, so the results would be back before they loaded the plane. The half-rack practice that morning was disciplined and well-executed. The players knew the game was on the horizon, and today was the last day the players would be in pads until they suited up to face Alabama. Coach Kelly applauded the team's preparation, then sent them off to the showers.

The parade of buses left the Gug and headed toward Corporate Wings South Bend. The team unloaded the buses, crossed off their names at the check-in table, and boarded the plane. In typical COVID fashion, the massive aircraft allowed the majority of the players to have an adjacent open seat. The trip occurred without incident, though the team flew into Alliance Field in Fort Worth rather than DFW to minimize the potential of an exposure.

REED: A few freshman walk-ons were squished into sets of three neighboring seats in the back. A plane large enough to allow everyone a vacant seat next to them would be costly. As traveling walk-ons in years prior, John and I were put in the same seats pressed together. So everyone poked fun at the young walk-ons as they experienced their traveling rite of passage.

Upon arrival, the players were reminded to set their watches an hour back and keep using their N95s until we reached the hotel. The Hilton Anatole hotel greeted each player with a thorny red rose. The welcome dinner took place in the Chantilly Ballroom East, a huge room with the tables the players had become used to at this point. The two-seater tables with name tags and plexiglass dividers spanned across the ballroom floor. The adjoining room, Chantilly Ballroom West, housed the player hospitality suite—a safe room for the players to pass the time. The room had seemingly endless snacks and drinks, numerous multiplayer arcade games, TVs to watch the other bowl games, massage chairs, and poker tables.

REED: Without fail, I was always blown away by the hospitality suites. Colorful lights shot across the rooms, and the shelves were filled to the brim with tasty treats. In addition to the playful amenities, every player was given a code to a website where they could pick their "bowl gifts." The site had hundreds of items to choose from. Some picked gifts for their friends and family; others chose things they wanted and probably wouldn't buy on their own. I chose two things my roommates and I could use back at our house in South Bend, an Amazon Fire TV Cube and a Hamilton Beach SoundShield blender. I received some backlash for the blender choice, but I stand by it.

The team awoke on the morning of Thursday, December 31—New Year's Eve—and attended Mass as a group, as they had before every game that season. The day's reading came from 1 John 2:18–21:

> Children, it is the last hour; and just as you heard that the antichrist was coming, so now many antichrists have appeared. Thus we know this is the last hour.
>
> They went out from us, but they were really not of our number; if they had been, they would have remained with us. Their desertion shows that none of them was of our number.
>
> But you have the anointing that comes from the Holy One, and you all have knowledge.
>
> I write to you not because you do not know the truth but because you do, and because every lie is alien to the truth.

The Gospel reading that followed came from the Book of John, and included a passage that read:

> The light shines in the darkness,
> and the darkness cannot overcome it.

Father Nate's homily was focused on these themes: togetherness, fortitude, and the conviction that can only come from overcoming significant adversity. There were very few people outside that room who believed the Irish had any chance the following afternoon—forcing them to rely on one another and the bonds that they'd created over the previous weeks, months, and years for strength and inspiration. Following communion, Robert Hainsey led the team in the Litany of the Blessed Virgin, appealing to the Blessed Mother for her protection and care in the hours and days that would follow.

JOHN: The readings and sermons at pregame Mass are often tailored to the week's events or the task at hand, but this one may have been even more pertinent given the circumstances. Father Nate did an excellent job of assuring and inspiring all of us of our conviction and belief in one another as we were forced to confront perhaps our most daunting challenge yet. Though we hoped it wouldn't be, the nature of a playoff is that every game can truly be the "last hour," just as the reading had said. In a moment when it seemed that there weren't many people who believed in us, the message was perfect. Everything up to that point—good or bad, triumphant or devastating, meticulously planned or entirely unexpected—had happened for a reason. The only people we truly needed on our journey were the ones already in the room with us, and everyone there—from the All-American to the student trainer—had a part to play in the drama that was certain to unfold the following afternoon.

Though it was a Thursday, the team treated it as a Focus Friday, meaning that practice that afternoon would be little more than a walk-through. The game plan was in place, and the team split up into position meetings to go over film and plays that they would see later in the day. From there, he team loaded the buses and traveled to Arlington for the first and last practice at AT&T Stadium before the game.

> **REED:** In 2018, when we faced Clemson in the Cotton Bowl, we arrived in Texas a week before the game and practiced every day in the stadium. Due to COVID, we were only allowed one practice in the stadium before the game.

A mix of post-traumatic stress and déjà vu hit the Irish as "Jerry World" came into view through the bus windows. After traveling through the long tunnel of twists and turns underneath the giant stadium, the buses halted in front of the team's locker room. The players found their lockers, changed into their kelly green walk-through gear, and walked out onto the field. The colossal jumbotron towered over the players as they ran through the call sheets against their respective scout teams. After Lea and Rees were confident in their unit's understanding of the game plan, Kelly huddled the team. He spoke of the importance of rest and confidence. One of the many signs that line the walls of the Gug says, "Confidence Is a Choice. Choose Confidence." He reiterated this mantra, sparking confidence within the players, and sent them off to the showers.

The players hit the showers and returned to the hotel. Meetings started up again after lunch, with special teams followed by offense and defense separately.

> **REED:** The defense had our game plan and schemes down pat. As I stood signaling at the front of the room, I noticed the lack of hesitation. There was an urgency to the players' answers. Not only did they want to prove to Lea that they knew the right answers, but they also wanted to reaffirm to every other player that they could trust them. A defense is only successful if every player works together, forming a cohesive unit.

At the time, Alabama had three contenders for the Heisman Trophy: wide receiver Devonta Smith, quarterback Mac Jones, and running back Najee Harris. Our game plan revolved heavily around shutting them down. Lea emphasized identifying where No. 6, Devonta Smith, was in the offensive formation before every snap. Although Smith was the clear choice for whom to contain, Alabama finished the regular season with five first-team All-Americans on their offense.

REED: I was confident in our game plan and preparation. Coach Lea had motivated the unit with the theme of redemption. We were coming off a difficult loss but were given a chance to prove that we belong. Lea reemphasized that Alabama had exceptional players all over the field, but we had everything we needed to get the job done.

JOHN: It was an incredibly reflective, self-aware meeting that evening. Coach Lea, in his characteristically thorough manner, went through where he thought we had gone wrong two weeks before in Charlotte. After the victory the first time around, he thought, we allowed emotion to get in the way—giving us a confidence heading into the second game that may have been misplaced. We lost our initial edge, he surmised, and when the margins are as small as they are in games like that, it can prove disastrous. In order to be successful the following day, he made clear that, for four quarters, we would need to focus more effectively and completely than we ever had before.

After meetings commenced, dinner was served in the ballroom. In the player hospitality suite, some players relaxed and watched football, others played poker, and a few gathered around the ping-pong and pool tables. This was the team's New Year's party. Some may have been saddened by the idea, but most of the team knew there were more important things than a ball drop and fireworks at stake.

> **REED:** For the second holiday in a row, I FaceTimed my family while they celebrated at a more traditional New Year's party. It was nice to see them having a good time. I remember them asking me if I was sad, sitting there alone in my hotel room. At that moment, would I rather have been at the beach celebrating? Yeah, probably. But would I have traded the unforgettable experience that would take place tomorrow for that? Absolutely not.

> **JOHN:** My hotel room provided a virtually unobstructed view of downtown Dallas, so I hoped I could at least see the midnight fireworks from afar. Unfortunately, it was too foggy to really make out much of anything.

On the morning of January 1, 2021, the Fighting Irish fueled up with a hearty breakfast and headed out to the parking garage for the pregame walk-through. The offense ran its plays against air on one side of the lot. On the other side, the defense faced a seasoned scout team offense running plays drawn out on an iPad—a sight one might not expect from a prestigious Division I football team heading into the College Football Playoff.

After a short break, the players changed into their travel suits, packed their rooms, and headed into their position meetings for the final round of film and questioning. At 11:40 AM, the team gathered in the Chantilly Ballroom for its pregame meal and team meeting. The players sat in silence as they ate—this time was meant for focus and reflection on everything they had studied and how they were going to execute during the game. Eventually, Coach Kelly took the stand at the front of the room. Kelly spoke on the gravity of this game. He emphasized playing with no regrets and leaving all effort and energy on the field. For some of the players in the room, this could be their last game in a Notre Dame jersey. There was no reason to hold anything back—the Irish needed a dominant performance.

It was a half-hour drive from the hotel to the stadium, which gave the team time to reflect before the afternoon's events. As the buses pulled into the tunnels beneath AT&T Stadium, it suddenly became very real for the Irish. Nineteen-point spread be damned. It was 0–0, and soon it would be time to play. After dropping their bags in the locker room, the defensive players headed to midfield—freshly painted with a Rose after hosting the Cotton Bowl just two days prior—and said their customary prayer. From there, they returned to the locker room to dress and took the field as the 18,373 approved fans began to file in.

At approximately 3:20 PM, the Alabama Crimson Tide kicked off to the Notre Dame Fighting Irish at AT&T Stadium in Arlington, Texas. It was the first Rose Bowl played outside Pasadena since 1942 and marked the first meeting between the two schools since the 2012 BCS Championship Game. After receiving the kick, Chris Tyree carried the ball out of the end zone to the 10-yard line, where he was ferociously introduced to Alabama's coverage unit. The ball was burst out of Tyree's clutches but was recovered by Notre Dame's Jack Kiser on the 8-yard line. After an impressive 15-yard run by Kyren Williams, the Irish were forced to punt.

JOHN: Going in, we knew that negative plays would kill us as we tried to execute our strategy. We got behind the chains there, and it cost us.

Following the punt, a pair of bruising runs by Najee Harris brought the Crimson Tide to the Notre Dame 26. On second down, Jones threw a quick pass to Devonta Smith running a bubble screen. The Irish defense appeared to be in position to make the play, but Smith's speed and twitch allow him to weave through Lewis and Hamilton virtually untouched. Alabama was up 7–0 after a commanding first drive.

> **REED:** It was no question; the first drive caught the team off guard. After a pair of fumbles from our offense and a lack of physicality from our defense, we knew we had to turn things around. The team was rattled.

On the next drive, the Irish made it to their own 44 before Book was stopped on third down. Bramblett's punt started Alabama's drive on the 3—a promising start for our defense. But Harris had other plans. On first down, Jones handed off to him in the end zone. He broke a few tackles and carried it for 15 yards. Two completed passes brought the Crimson Tide to the Alabama 35. On the ensuing snap, Harris went viral, creating a play that aired on *SportsCenter*'s "Top Plays" repeatedly for the next few weeks. Jones handed the ball off to Harris for what looked like a loss of yards. Harris was locked up in the backfield until an opening presented itself. He took the ball outside, where he was greeted head-on by Irish cornerback Nick McCloud. Did Harris dive inside and try to truck through the rest of the defense for a few extra yards? Did he take the few positive yards and run out of bounds? No, he ran directly at McCloud and leapt into the air. McCloud had lowered his head, expecting contact, allowing Harris to hurdle right over him. Harris caught his balance smoothly and proceeded to run downfield before being knocked out of bounds at the Notre Dame 12-yard line.

REED: Najee Harris's hurdle happened about two yards in front of John and me on the sideline. I remember time standing still for a moment as the behemoth of a man floated four feet in the air right in front of my eyes. I couldn't believe it. After a large offensive gain, I normally sprint down the field to be parallel with the defense so they can see me. This time, I just stood there trying to comprehend what had occurred. John gave me a slight shove. I blinked my eyes, picked my jaw up off the ground, and ran downfield.

JOHN: I'd never seen anything quite like that, because it wasn't as if Nick dove at his ankles. Harris had to have been at least three feet off the ground. Though I was equally as stunned, I could sense that Alabama was going to attempt to run another play pretty quickly and take advantage of our relative disorganization.

A miscommunication on defense left tight end Jahleel Billingsley wide open in the end zone for a touchdown the next play. Harris' acrobatics led to another quick scoring drive by the Crimson Tide, leaving the Fighting Irish down by 14.

After a touchback, a determined Notre Dame offense took the field. Chris Tyree used his speed to cover 27 yards before being tackled on the Alabama 45. After a timeout, Coach Rees put the ball in Kyren Williams' hands nine times out of the next 12 plays. After an eight-minute, 15-play drive, Williams hammered into the end zone from one yard out. It was clear Notre Dame's game plan involved a heavy run game and killing as much time as possible. But it had worked. The Irish had cut the lead to seven.

REED: The play before, I would have sworn that Book had made it into the end zone. From my angle, as well as the views the jumbotron showed, Book seemed to have possession as he crossed the endline. The referees thought otherwise. That being said, I was happy Kyren was able to get the points. He had given everything he had on that drive and was very deserving of the recognition.

The next drive looked encouraging for the Fighting Irish defense. For the first three plays, the Irish allowed less than five yards and managed to give Alabama their first third down of the game—providing the first legitimate opportunity for the ND defense to get off the field. Unfortunately, the Tide offense wouldn't cooperate. The following three plays couldn't have been more different than the first three. On third down, Devonta Smith caught a bubble pass and took the ball 24 yards across the 50. With Shaun Crawford in perfect defensive positioning, Jahleel Billingsley caught what appeared to be the uncatchable for a 15-yard gain. Then, with the Irish defense on its heels, Mac Jones connected with Devonta Smith on a slant, who blew past the Irish secondary for a 34-yard touchdown to make it 21–7.

When Book and the offense retook the field, Alabama came rearranged and ready. They had adjusted to Notre Dame's offensive game plan and were now blatantly showing heavy run protection. Their linebackers played closer to the line of scrimmage, the defensive line predicted run blocks, and their secondary had shifted down. The arrangements were successful. Despite a third-down conversion catch by George Takacs, the drive ultimately stalled. After six plays and 18 yards, the Irish were forced to punt. Tuscaloosa native Jay Bramblett came on for the third time that afternoon, hoping to continue his momentum after recording two 50-yard punts earlier in the game. This kick, however, only traveled 34 yards before sailing out of bounds, giving the Tide the ball on their own 23.

To start the drive, Jones handed the ball off to Najee Harris, who barreled down the field for a gain of seven. Drew White brought down Harris on first down, while Jeremiah Owusu-Karamoah tackled him on second, forcing a third-and-1. Aligning under center, Jones snuck up the middle for three yards, gaining a new set of downs. Again Alabama fed Harris, but the Irish were beginning to look more confident and aggressive. On first down, Shayne Simon sliced through the offensive line, stuffing Harris for a short gain. On second down, Mac Jones threw a screen pass to Harris behind the line of scrimmage, allowing Drew White and a host of Irish defenders to stop Harris in his tracks. After a first-down pass to Devonta Smith, the Irish were adamant about restraining Alabama here. Harris was held to a gain of three on the next play. Jones nervously flipped the ball to Smith after a close call with Notre Dame's Myron Tagovailoa-Amosa. Smith attempted to take the ball outside, setting up a meeting between the recently crowned Biletnikoff and Butkus Award winners in the flat. Despite Smith's success earlier in the game, this round went to Owusu-Koramoah as he and Hamilton escorted him out of bounds for a loss of five. The Irish forced Alabama to use a timeout on third-and-12. A hurried Mac Jones threw the ball out of bounds. The pass was intended for Metchie, who was well guarded by Irish corner Nick McCloud. The incomplete pass brought fourth down on the Alabama 44-yard line and caused Alabama's punter to take the field for the first time.

REED: This was a massive moment for our team. It proved Alabama was human and we could stop them. Drew White and Wu were playing free and fast and meeting the running backs in the backfield. Crawford and Hamilton were playing with confidence and hitting hard. I could tell Lea had noticed these changes from the tone in his voice. There was less hesitation in his play call—he knew the players had settled in and were able to execute his calls. There was never a dull moment on the headsets. Either Lea and Elston were rapidly discussing defensive line fronts and rushes, or Lea was putting Coach Kelly at ease, who jumped over from the offensive channel. I remember a few times where I had trouble hearing Lea's play call through the commotion and had to make some educated guesses. Thankfully, I never guessed wrong.

JOHN: After having to adjust to Bama's speed, talent, and scheme on the first few drives, it felt like we'd finally settled in. Obviously, we'd dug a bit of a hole for ourselves, but there was a growing sense on our sideline that we'd have a shot at this one if a few things broke our way in the second half.

Notre Dame took the field with 44 seconds left in the half. After a nine-yard scramble on first down, Book gained 20 yards right up the middle on a quarterback draw. Two plays later, Book found Skowronek for another 20-yard gain. The tempo offense was working well for the Irish, as seconds ticked off the game clock. With 19 seconds left in the half, the Irish spiked the ball to stop the clock. With one timeout left, Kelly decided to throw to get Jon Doerer, his kicker, in range. After a loss on first down, Williams stepped out of bounds at the Alabama 33, setting up a 51-yard field-goal attempt. This kick would have tied Doerer's career longest kick—set just two weeks before in the ACC Championship Game. Unfortunately, the ball was deflected by Alabama's Will Anderson, causing it to fall short of the uprights. Jones took a knee, and both teams ran back through their tunnels.

REED: Our team was extraordinary. Our locker room at halftime, although seemingly hectic, was full of productive communication, bolstering confidence in one another and genuine belief in our plan. Lea collected Drew and Bo's observations and used them to help shift our game plan in the right direction. The strong bonds between coaches and players helped make our halftimes so incredibly valuable. As Nick read his notes to Coach Lea, who wrote them out on the whiteboard, I peered around the room. Every player listened intently to the coaches without breaking eye contact. The intensity of their focus made me ask myself what I was doing, and I quickly focused back on Coach Lea. Our game plan was working; it just took some time. We were stopping the runs and executing precise pass drops. Defensively, our last drive was flawless. We just needed to keep our awareness high, track No. 6, and play physical football.

Associate athletic director Ron Powlus dragged some of the coaches from their meeting areas in typical halftime fashion and sent them back up to the box. The players took a knee in front of Coach Kelly, eager to get back on the field. Kelly shouted, "Juice!" They needed energy in the locker room. Players smiled and lifted their heads higher. Kelly proclaimed that Alabama is not the Goliath the team had been described to be. It was important to Kelly that the players knew that they could win this game, and it wouldn't take a miracle. He reemphasized the team's traits, as well as the fact that this particular group of Fighting Irish was like no other group in Notre Dame history or anywhere else in the country. This band of brothers was "built different," he insisted. Everything the Irish needed to win was right there, in that locker room.

JOHN: It felt dramatically different than the locker room at the Cotton Bowl two years before. That time, guys were really upset, and it created a tension that I don't think helped us in the second half. This time, everything was more measured. Obviously, we had some ground to cover, but everyone understood that, despite taking a few punches, we still found ourselves in a spot where we weren't completely out of it yet.

Billingsley fair caught Doerer's kickoff to start the second half. A few plays in, Jones connected with a leaping Devonta Smith, bringing the Crimson Tide out to the 50-yard-line. The Fighting Irish defense had been improving in stopping the run game, but after three consecutive Harris runs, Alabama still managed to gain the first down. However, on the next set of downs, Harris was met by Owusu-Koramoah in the backfield on first down, causing a dropped pass, and met again by Drew White and Marist Liufau on second— forcing a third-and-11. Jones snapped the ball and dropped back to pass, but Notre Dame's Jayson Ademilola, fighting through two Alabama offensive linemen, got his arm up in the air to deflect Jones' pass. The ball ricocheted off Ademilola's arm and back into the hands of Jones. Ademilola powered through the offensive guard and tackled Jones, forcing a fourth down and a loss of yards.

REED: The defensive coaches knew Alabama would be running the ball to start the half. They were up by 14 and were going to try to run the clock out. Lea knew this and continuously called run-heavy defensive schemes. The perfect calls and execution led to a third-and-long where Lea had us send out the "penny" group. Expecting a pass, we ambushed the offensive line upfront and had great coverage in the back, allowing Jayson to make a magnificent play. Not only did he deflect the pass and sack the quarterback, but he may have brought Alabama out of field-goal range as well. The headset channel was ecstatic—a fantastic start to the half.

A diving catch by Skowronek brought the Irish out to the 16-yard line after a deep punt was fair caught by Matt Salerno. After a few short gains, Book connected with Michael Mayer, the standout freshman tight end, for a 10-yard gain. Though they were still in their own territory, visions of a one-score game began to dance in the heads of the Notre Dame faithful. But the promising start was abruptly halted when Book, looking for Mayer again, was intercepted by Alabama's cornerback Christian Harris.

REED: Michael Mayer had an exceptional first year. He is a very nice guy with an impressive knowledge of the game. His skill and maturity had a strong impact on our offense. Mayer's maneuverability after the catch is what makes him truly special. After his success on the field, he earned the nickname "Baby Gronk" among some journalists.

JOHN: You could definitely sense a shift in momentum after we managed the stop, and it only intensified as the offense moved the ball down the field. We'd started the half about as well as we could have expected to, so it's just a shame to have turned the ball over like that. Ian did an excellent job of evading pressure and throwing on the run, but it was just a touch short—and the kid from Alabama made an excellent play on it.

The Irish defense took the field, looking to replicate the results from their last drive. Jones snapped the ball at the Alabama 38 with other plans in mind. Throwing over the middle, he completed a pass to wide receiver John Metchie, who ran all the way down to the Notre Dame 22. The following play, a 10-yard holding penalty was called on an Alabama offensive lineman. This is the first penalty on either team this game—a remarkable feat that highlights the intense discipline of all players on the field. On second down, Drew White made a diving tackle at Harris' legs, causing a third-and-4. Great coverage enabled the defensive line to push Jones out of the pocket, but he escaped downfield and collected the first down. Devonta Smith finished off the drive with a seven-yard touchdown reception. His third score of the game, the catch was made at the pylon with both feet just barely in bounds and may well have cemented his already probable Heisman victory just a few days later.

The Fighting Irish, now down 28–7, took the touchback and began their drive on the 25. On second down, Alabama received a 15-yard roughing-the-passer penalty, leading to first-and-10. Unfortunately, they were unable to capitalize on the Tide's mistake. On the next snap, Book couldn't escape Alabama's four-man rush and was sacked for a loss of 14. Alabama defensive tackle Christian Barmore not only got the sack but crushed Book with his 311-pound body. Drew Pyne, Notre Dame's true freshman backup quarterback, was subbed in as a result. He completed an on-target pass to Skowronek for seven yards but was well short of the first down.

> **REED:** Book is a strong, gritty player who can take a hit, so seeing him down was a worrying sight, to say the least. Watching big hits on television or even from the stands does not begin to give the real impacts justice. I've seen Book get banged, squished, and pounded, and he popped right back up every time. This hit was different. It had been a long game so far, but if anyone was able to shake it off and get back out there next drive, it was him.

The Irish were forced to punt once again, and Smith brought back the Bramblett kick for a 20-yard return. Immediately, two big passes to Alabama's Slade Bolden and Miller Forristall brought the Crimson Tide to the Notre Dame 44-yard line. The whistle blew, signaling the end of the third quarter. After the teams flipped sides, the final quarter of the 2021 Rose Bowl began. Harris started the quarter with a 13-yard run to cap off an impressive game. Notre Dame showed its unwavering spirit with an aggressive rush on the following play, and Shayne Simon batted down Jones' pass. Next, Jones handed off to running back Brian Robinson Jr., who met White, Owusu-Koramoah, and Cross at the line of scrimmage. On third-and-8, Hamilton raced toward an open Billingsley, who caught the pass, but was stopped in his tracks, forcing Alabama to settle for a field goal. The drive was an extraordinary display of heart and determination by the Irish defense, unwilling to back off.

JOHN: It would have been really easy for a number of guys— particularly those who knew they'd be entering the draft that spring—to take their foot off the gas at this point. It says a tremendous amount about them that they continued to fight and stayed competitive through the fourth quarter against one of the best offenses college football has ever seen.

Thankfully, Ian Book retook the field to finish off his final season on his feet. Book connected with Javon McKinley, who used his height and size to tap the ball up to himself and stay in bounds for a gain of 18. From there, Williams powered through the Alabama defensive line for another first down. Two passes to "Baby Gronk" Michael Mayer, one for seven yards, the other for 18, brought the Irish to the Alabama 13-yard line. Once again,

Book found Michael Mayer, this time in the end zone. With just over 10 minutes to play, the Irish offense suddenly showed signs of life. Sadly, the play was called back due to an illegal shift, costing the Irish the touchdown and an additional five yards. From the Alabama 18, Book and the offense were then unable to score in their four attempts. Book threw short of Avery Davis on fourth down, causing a turnover on downs.

> **REED:** I remember celebrating Michael's touchdown zealously until I saw the yellow bird fly through the air. Confused, I switched over to the offensive channel to hear what the coaches were saying. At the flick of the switch, I quickly had to turn down the volume as I heard Kelly squawking at the ref over the call. Supposedly, Chris Tyree hadn't set his feet on the line of scrimmage after running in motion. The call had zero bearings on the play's outcome, angering myself and those around me even further. Either way, I was happy we went for it on fourth down a few plays later. It proved the resilience and attitude that this team was built on.

With excellent starting position, the Fighting Irish defense took the field to face Alabama at their own 14. On first down, Metchie caught Jones' pass and ran the ball out another 10 yards. After an Alabama false-start penalty, the Irish held Robinson Jr. to a gain of six. On second-and-9, Jones completed a pass to Williams for no gain. Lea, wanting to send a message, blitzed Owusu-Koramoah and Bauer. The rush by Owusu-Koramoah, Bauer, and Ogundeji startled Jones, forcing him to throw the ball away. The sheer speed and aggression of the blitz made Jones throw the ball frantically. With not one Crimson Tide player in the area, the referee called intentional grounding, leading to a fourth-and-17—a meaningful victory for the Irish defense.

With 5:25 left in the fourth quarter, Book and the offense started the drive. A 20-yard completion to Lawrence Keys III brought the Irish to their own 43. After a short run by Tyree, a sack, and an incomplete pass to Mayer, Kelly sent out the punt unit on fourth-and-8. Shortly after, Kelly called a timeout. With nothing to lose, Kelly decided to send his offense back out onto the field instead. Then Book found Avery Davis for his first catch of the day, for 15 yards and a first down.

> **REED:** John and I agreed that there was no point in punting at this point—we might as well go out swinging.

> **JOHN:** Particularly since we'd come so close on the last drive, we felt like we owed it to ourselves to keep pushing. The odds of a comeback were probably prohibitively long at that point, but we hadn't gotten this far by giving up.

On what most onlookers assumed would be the Irish's final drive, Book overthrew Skowronek on first down. The ball landed in the hands of Alabama cornerback Patrick Surtain II, but he was ruled out of bounds. Flags flew on the other side of the field as head coach Nick Saban was called for an unsportsmanlike-conduct penalty. Saban screamed vehemently at the referee across the field while standing five yards off the sideline. Clearly, both Kelly and Saban, no matter the score, were coaching until the final whistle. A catch by Mayer downed the ball on the Alabama 13. While off balance, Williams made an acrobatic catch and ran the ball to the 8. In an attempt to finish the drive, Book reached Mayer on a pivot route one yard short of the end zone. With 56 seconds left in the game, Book faked the handoff and ran untouched into the end zone—a perfect end to a four-and-a-half minute, 14 play, 80-yard drive.

To maintain Notre Dame's unyielding attitude, the Fighting Irish sent out their onside kickoff unit. Doerer executed the kick perfectly, making it virtually impossible to catch. The ball skipped off of Devonta Smith's chest and was snatched out of the air by the Butkus Award winner, Jeremiah Owusu-Koramoah, on his final play of the night.

> **REED:** Wu truly has one speed. It didn't matter if we were down by 50 or up by 50—if Wu was on the field, he was giving everything he had. It was an honor to work with him every day and watch him play up close.

A few short passes and a pair of long runs by Book brought the Irish to the Alabama 15 with one second left. On the final play, Alabama ran an all-out blitz, hurrying Book to get the ball out of his hands. The ball stumbled short of its target, and the Rose Bowl clock struck zero.

The players from both sides hugged their teammates and then united on the field to congratulate each other. The Notre Dame players exited the field and headed back into the locker room. They didn't know it at the time, but they'd held the Tide to their lowest point total in nearly two seasons. Alabama was moving on—they'd go on to dominate Ohio State and earn their sixth national title in the last 12 seasons. For the Irish, it marked the second time in the last three seasons that their season ended at the hands of the eventual national champions.

> **JOHN:** Alabama's brilliance was undeniable, and I had no qualms about referring to them as the best team I'd ever seen. It didn't do much to lift my spirits, but it wasn't as if we'd lost to a team that we felt like didn't deserve it.

In the locker room, everyone sat quietly in front of their lockers. They waited for Kelly and the coaches up in the box to make their way down. Some players began to undress. It was easy to tell who was a senior and who was not. Every senior sat there in full pads cherishing the moment, knowing this was the last time they would ever wear the blue and gold jersey. Coach Kelly arrived, and the players knelt down around him. He was proud to have coached this team. This team was different, and every player in the room knew it. Kelly said that he spoke with Saban after the game. Kelly told him he thought about not attempting the onside kick but realized it would not be doing this team, who had fought so hard and been through so much together, justice. Saban responded that he was glad they went for it—he expected nothing less from Notre Dame than to fight until the final whistle blew. This team was never going to give up, from Book getting back in the game after an injury, to Wu recovering the onside kick with a few seconds left. This game perfectly exemplified our team's characteristics. The Irish had been through so much to get to this point. Whether it was adjusting to COVID-19 regulations or being down in games earlier in the season, the Irish were never going to give in, and that was something to be proud of.

The players broke into their position groups. Tears were shed, hugs were given, and well-wishes were shared with those who had played their last game for Notre Dame.

Coach Lea struggled to speak to his defense as he gazed toward the glossy red eyes staring back at him. As the next head coach at his alma mater, Vanderbilt, this was his final game in Irish colors as well. He ensured every player that although he was leaving Notre Dame, he would always be a resource for anything the players needed, just a phone call away.

REED: My Notre Dame football career ended at that moment. I embraced my teammates and coaches and wished them luck in the next year. I saw some players around me bawling their eyes out. I was sad but was able to hold myself together in the locker room. I thought I was going to make it through the night without crying. I was wrong. It wasn't until I met my parents and brother outside the stadium that I started crying. It was the weirdest thing—I remember laughing at myself while trying to hide my face behind my hat and my mother's shoulder. We had put so much hard time and effort into this team over the last few years, and it had finally come to an end. There were no more 5:00 AM workouts, no more pitch-black, below-freezing practices, and no more stadium sprints under the blazing sun. Eventually, I pulled myself together. I chatted with my family and the families around us—it had been a while since I had last seen them—and then boarded the buses with the rest of the team.

As Ohio State handily defeated Clemson in the Sugar Bowl, setting up a Buckeyes–Crimson Tide matchup in the national title game, the 2020 Notre Dame Fighting Irish quietly rode to Fort Worth. From there, a group that had accomplished a tremendous amount and been through so much together boarded the plane back to South Bend for the final time, marking the end of a season to remember.

EPILOGUE

On the morning of January 2, the Irish awoke to frigid temperatures and several new inches of snow on the ground in South Bend. The season—one that many doubted would ever occur—was over, and outside of the perfunctory set of good-byes and a to-go meal at the Gug, there wasn't much else to be said or done. The underclassmen—a group that included All-Americans Kyle Hamilton and Kyren Williams, as well as freshman All-American Michael Mayer—would be back the following month to start the entire process over again, but for the senior class, it was a premature end to a truly remarkable run. The Class of '21 joined the team immediately after the 4–8 debacle in 2016 but had gone 43–8, only lost once at home in their four years on campus, recorded two undefeated regular seasons and College Football Playoff appearances, and won 10 or more games in four consecutive years for the first time in program history. And though some of them would be returning for a fifth year, this was it for the majority of a group that had helped vault Notre Dame Football back into national relevance.

The guys who wouldn't be coming back needed to clean out their lockers—a task made more challenging by the COVID-19 protocols that forced some of them to dress at the stadium. Their shoes, gloves, and other practice-related items were kept at the IAC, so they collected those before heading into the game day locker room for what they assumed would be their final visit. Name plates were removed and saved for posterity, pictures were taken, and duffel bags were filled with mementos of a four-year journey that seemed to have begun just yesterday. As a few of them turned to finally leave, they noticed that the tunnel door was left slightly ajar. Not quite ready to leave, they investigated further, finding that the path to the field was virtually unobstructed. Naturally, then, they headed down the steps, slapping the PLAY LIKE A CHAMPION TODAY sign once more before finding themselves in the tunnel.

> **JOHN:** Someone had made an attempt to cordon off the field, but we weren't going to be stopped that easily. It's easy to romanticize the notion of "saying good-bye" to something that was an important part of your life for so long, but I think most of us felt like we'd earned those few extra minutes.

> **REED:** From the tunnel's top, we could see the fresh white snow blanketing the field. It seemed inviting. It was cold, and we were all unprepared, but it didn't much matter. Few words were exchanged—just a nod in that direction was enough to draw this group of washed-up seniors onto the field for one last private farewell.

Once there, they were confronted with a snow-covered playing surface. Idyllic as though it might have been, they'd come wearing tennis shoes and thus were unprepared to take the field. Undeterred, they made the journey to the 50-yard-line (or close to it), where—after a period of deliberation—they decided to take advantage of the winter weather and leave a parting gift from the 2021 class of Notre Dame walk-ons.

Barely 10 minutes later, a full-size snowman had appeared near the stadium's south end zone. With two rolls of tape for eyes, an unchewed gumball for a nose, and a team-issued COVID mask covering his mouth, it was simultaneously absurd and completely fitting.

> **JOHN:** It sounds juvenile—I completely understand. In our defense, however, it was just one of those irreverent things that everyone does at one time or another in college. Some of us were done with school entirely, but all of us silently understood that this was truly a last grasp at a time in our lives that we'd remember forever but were now being forced to leave behind. Suddenly, we were ex–football players, and I guess we needed to feel like we could leave one more mark on a place that had provided us with so many memories over the years.

> **REED:** Yes, our WOPU class of 2021 senior gift would melt away, but the memory will never fade, and we will always look back on our time in the golden helmet with pride and honor. We can only hope that our impression, although modest, may bolster the tradition of Notre Dame football for seasons to come.

After a few photos, the cold wore the group down. No tears were shed as the players left the field for the last time and ultimately went their separate ways. The months and years before had been simultaneously thrilling and heartbreaking, monotonous and unforgettable, incredibly taxing yet immeasurably rewarding. In that time, they'd become men of Notre Dame, each in his own distinct way. And though their names, at least as far as football was concerned, would quickly be relegated to the dustbin of history, they shared a steadfast understanding that they had seen, experienced, and in some instances created that very history firsthand.

ACKNOWLEDGMENTS

It would be impossible to properly thank everyone who helped us make this project a reality, but we'd be remiss if we didn't mention a select few who truly allowed this idea to come to life.

First and foremost, we'd like to thank the Triumph Books team—Josh, Noah, Adam, Alex, Jesse, and so many others—who took a chance on a couple of washed-up former walk-ons who thought they had an interesting story to tell. They've turned this project into so much more than we ever could have imagined, and for that we are incredibly grateful.

Second, we'd like to thank everyone within the Notre Dame football program who helped us with photos, interviews, and all the ancillary things that made this project what it is. We'd like to give a special thanks to Katy Lonergan and Hunter Bivin for helping us navigate through university departments, licensing regulations, and virtually every other roadblock we never could have anticipated when we first started. Additionally, we'd like to thank Coach Brian Kelly for his leadership throughout the season, as well as his generosity in agreeing to write the foreword.

To our teammates and coaches on the 2020 Fighting Irish—thank you for everything. Each and every one of you played an enormous role in last season's journey, and we hope that this book serves as a reminder of a shared experience that none of us will ever forget.

To the men of WOPU Nation (and 417 Napoleon)—it was an honor to take this journey with each and every one of you. You were sounding boards, drinking buddies, and the most loyal teammates and friends that anyone could have ever imagined. The

Nation is stronger than ever, and it's been the honor of a lifetime to call ourselves WOPU men.

We'd also like to thank Joe Gregory—Reed's uncle—for his valuable assistance in editing our manuscript.

Additionally, we'd like to recognize Nick Lezynski, Chris O'Leary, Matt Salerno, Max Siegel, Abbie Martin, GP Pernicone, Grace Hachigian, Fr. Nate Wills, and everyone else we spoke with during the creative process for being generous enough with their time to allow us to interview them. Each and every one of your stories added a tremendous amount to our narrative, and we could not have made it what it was without your patience and generosity.

Of course, we'd also like to thank our immediate families for their support not only throughout our athletic endeavors but also throughout our entire lives. You've given us the strength, inspiration, and ability to dream big and achieve things that we never could have imagined, and for that we are indescribably grateful.

Finally, we wanted to thank the Notre Dame Class of 2021. One of the most unique things about Notre Dame, in our estimation, is that it's impossible to extricate football from the day-to-day student experience. It's not an exaggeration to say that, from early September through the end of the semester, the entire campus lives and breathes football. And though 2020—our senior year—presented a tremendous number of challenges, your passion and commitment to our team and university never wavered. You shared in our struggles, uncertainties, triumphs, and disappointments, and this story is as much yours as it is either of ours. Love thee forever.